Listening to the Parables of Jesus

Jesus Seminar Guides

Bernard Brandon Scott, series editor

Published volumes

Listening to the Parables of Jesus

Edward F. Beutner, editor

POLEBRIDGE PRESS
Santa Rosa, California

Cover and interior design by Robaire Ream

Library of Congress Cataloging-in-Publication Data

Listening to the parables of Jesus / edited by Edward F. Beutner.
    p. cm. -- (Jesus seminar guides ; v. 2)
  Includes bibliographical references.
  ISBN-13: 978-1-59815-003-2
  1. Jesus Christ--Parables. I. Beutner, Edward F.
  BT375.3.L57 2007
  226.8'06--dc22

                                                    2007032422

Table of Contents

Series Preface

Westar Institute, the home of the Jesus Seminar, is an advocate
for literacy in religion and the Bible. A member-supported,
non-profit research and educational institute, its mission is to
foster collaborative research in religious studies and to communicate the results of the scholarship of religion to a broad,
non-specialist public. Through publications, educational pro-
grams, and research projects like the Jesus Seminar, Westar
brings Fellows of the Institute—scholars with advanced
degrees in biblical studies, religion, or related fields—into conversation with non-specialists from all walks of life.

Westar's series, *Jesus Seminar Guides*, is designed to gather
the best writings of Westar Fellows from the pages of its mem-
bership magazine, *The Fourth R,* its academic journal,
Forum, and occasionally from previously unpublished material. Arranged topically, the *Guides* summarize the important
questions and debates that have driven the work of the Jesus
Seminar over the last twenty years. They are intended for use
in classrooms, discussion groups inside and outside churches,
and for the general reader.

Contributors

Edward F. Beutner has served in pastoral and academic assignments in Wisconsin and in California. A poet and member of the Scholars Version translation committee, he specializes in the rhetorical analysis and translation of the parables, aphorisms, and other metaphorical language found in New Testament texts. He has taught comparative religion at Nicolet College in Wisconsin; and biblical studies, philosophy and literature at Ohlone College, Las Positas College, and at Santa Rosa Junior College in northern California.

Robert W. Funk was a distinguished teacher, writer, translator, and publisher in the field of religion. A Guggenheim Fellow and Senior Fulbright Scholar, he served as Annual Professor of the American School of Oriental Research in Jerusalem and as chair of the Graduate Department of Religion at Vanderbilt University. Robert Funk was a recognized pioneer in modern biblical scholarship, having led the Society of Biblical Literature as its Executive Secretary from 1968–1973. His many books include *The Five Gospels: The Search for the Authentic Words of Jesus* (1993) and *The Acts of Jesus: The Search for the Authentic Deeds* (1998)—both with the Jesus Seminar—as well as *Honest to Jesus* (1996), and *A Credible Jesus* (2002).

Lane C. McGaughy is the Geo. H. Atkinson Professor of Religious and Ethical Studies emeritus at Willamette University in Salem, Oregon. He is the author of two books and numerous scholarly articles in academic journals and anthologies. The former president and executive secretary of the Pacific Northwest Region of the American Academy of Religion and Society of Biblical Literature, he worked with his mentor, Robert W. Funk, on a series of projects, including a Greek grammar, the establishment of the Religious Studies Department at the University of Montana, the founding of

Scholars Press, the development of Polebridge Press and Westar Institute, and the reorganization of the Society of Biblical Literature. Dr. McGaughy is an ordained United Methodist minister.

Robert J. Miller is the Associate Professor of Religious Studies at Juniata College in Pennsylvania. A Fellow of the Jesus Seminar since 1986, he was Scholar-in-Residence at Westar Institute in 2001. In addition to having edited *The Complete Gospels* (1992), an anthology of twenty early gospels presented in Westar's innovative translation, the Scholars Version, he is the author of *The Jesus Seminar and Its Critics* (1999) and *Born Divine* (2003).

Bernard Brandon Scott is the Darbeth Distinguished Professor of New Testament at the Phillips Theological Seminary, Tulsa, Oklahoma. He is the author of several books, including *Re-Imagine the World* (2002), *Hear Then the Parable* (1989), and *Hollywood Dreams and Biblical Stories* (1994). With Robert Funk and James R. Butts, he co-edited *The Parables of Jesus: Red Letter Edition* (1988), the first report of the Jesus Seminar; co-authored *Reading New Testament Greek* with a group of students (1993); and edited *Funk on Parables*, collection of essays by Robert W. Funk (2006).

Paul Verhoeven is a film director and a longtime member of the Jesus Seminar. He has a Ph.D. in Physics and Mathematics from the University of Leiden. His film credits include *Black Book, Robocop, Total Recall, Basic Instinct*, and *Starship Troopers*.

Introduction

The Haunt of Parable

Edward F. Beutner

W hat if the purpose or function of a parable is not to instruct but to haunt? Keep this question in mind as you explore the individual essays in this book. Notice how from time to time its scholarly contributors scratch their heads in puzzlement over the yin and yang of Jesus' parables.

To get down to the brass tacks of Jesus' parables is to begin with a terse description of that which all his parables have in common. Contemporary scholars find it hard to improve on this brief sketch by C. H. Dodd, a Welsh parable scholar of the mid-twentieth century:

> At its simplest the parable is a metaphor or simile,
> drawn from nature or common life,
> arresting the listener
> by its vividness or strangeness—
> and leaving the mind in sufficient doubt
> about its precise application
> to tease it into active thought.
>
> —Dodd, *Parables of the Kingdom*, p. 5

Robert W. Funk once termed Dodd's essential insight as "recognizing the rhetorical register of the text." Funk's essay in this present volume offers several telling glimpses of Jesus as a religious genius and storytelling sage. He invites the reader to hear in the language of Jesus the Galilean peasant the same twists and turns, irony and suspense, hyperbole, humor, and wit that is characteristic of all enduring storytellers. Once modern readers grasp the metaphor and imagination in Jesus' stories (as some of his earliest listeners must surely have done), then an assent to the *poetics* of his speech can open the door to the surprising impact of parable as non-literal language, orally performed.

Although parables are poetic, Funk is careful to distinguish them from the kind of romantic or escapist poetry that transports us away from this world toward some safe haven of a future never-never land. On the contrary, parables focus our attention ever more closely upon this world . . . and then suddenly disconnect its accustomed dots and disorder its rigid boundaries. During the parable we as listeners/participants re-envision this actual world in wholly unaccustomed ways— even in ways that seem contrary to what we ordinarily take to be our better judgment. Jesus' parables routinely frustrate our inherited expectations by means of narrative twists that reflect what Funk names "the logic of grace."

"The logic of grace," may, in fact, best describe the single recurring theme of the otherwise quite distinctive essays in this book. They all disclose a paradox that faces scholars and non-scholars alike: we set out to interpret the parable and find the parable interprets us. We stand before parables as hitters stand in the batter's box facing Greg Maddux: too sure of ourselves on the one hand, or acknowledging our befuddlement on the other. The parables provide the grace of befuddlement; what happens after that is hard to say.

Lane McGaughy's opening essay provides high fidelity earphones that alert readers to hear the vivid and distinctive nature of the language of parable. McGaughy spells out for us how the language of parable operates; how its formal structure and design affects the listener inwardly; and how the art of close listening can contribute to the import, force, and surprise of the narrative itself. His essay "Jesus' Parables and the Fiction of the Kingdom" re-echoes the wry smile and wise caveat of a Billy Collins poem entitled "Introduction to Poetry":

I ask them to take a poem
and hold it up to the light
like a color slide

or press an ear against its hive.

I say drop a mouse into a poem
and watch him probe his way out,

or walk inside the poem's room
and feel the walls for a light switch.

I want them to waterski
across the surface of a poem
waving at the author's name on the shore.

But all they want to do
is tie the poem to a chair with rope
and torture a confession out of it.

They begin beating it with a hose
to find out what it really means.

McGaughy's essay figuratively invites its readers to hold the fiction of parable up to the reliable light of their own personal and communal experience, and to take off their actual shoes to waterski—barefoot if they dare—across the parable's surface.

To stay with the Billy Collins poem for a moment: Robert Miller, Brandon Scott, Paul Verhoeven, and I have each dropped a mouse or two of our own into the parables that we explore. I identify a number of poetic devices and possibilities within the parables, and show how these features can have a refractory and astonishing effect upon the listener. I have attempted to exercise the kind of reader-response criticism that takes seriously Funk's dictum that parables should interpret the listener, and not the other way around. And while unraveling a number of parables for the reader, I have at the same time allowed these parables to unravel *me* in the presence of the reader.

Robert Miller offers an original and extensive treatment of two parables that appear in the gospels of Matthew and Thomas, narratives that Miller renames "The Overpriced Pearl" and "The Treasure of Immorality." His essay makes a careful and persuasive case that these two parables very likely reflect concrete situations in the life and times of Jesus, and thus might well reveal an autobiographical dimension worth examining more closely.

With his director's eye for narrative structure, Paul Verhoeven identifies some fault lines in Matthew's version of the Vineyard Laborers, and proposes an alternate version, which he considers more likely to have come from Jesus. Then Miller engages Verhoeven in a discussion about his proposal; their lively exchange of views provides the reader with a brief but representative sample of the candor and civility with which arguments typically progress in the deliberations of the Jesus Seminar.

In his essay on the Leased Vineyard, Brandon Scott demonstrates how insights from a rabbinic parable can illuminate for us the otherwise shadowy nooks and crannies of a dark parable of violence found in Mark's gospel. In Scott's final essay, he has rightly identified Jesus' parables as rooted in the Wisdom Tradition of Israel. The parables stand in the tradition of that segment of wisdom stories which regard everything as sacred ("God is nowhere absent, everywhere hidden")—a banal truism unless it constitutes an overall vision and governs everyday behavior, as it did for Jesus. Scott suggests that the *denominated* sacred (persons, places, things) can no longer posture for status, privilege, or dominance over against the disinherited nobodies and outcasts; or at least not in the name of the Holy. Scott applauds "the reappearance of parable" in current biblical studies. In it he credits Jesus with disturbing the false, oppressive 'peace' of Empire through the art of terse, irreverent, and highly poetic storytelling.

Beutner, Funk and Scott offer three final essays which describe the parables globally as artful language events—as prominent fulcrums, so to speak, upon which our inherited or 'default' understanding of the world gets overturned and undermined. Even if at first hearing the parables might grate against our ears like chalk against blackboard, all three authors argue that studying the parables will redound to our advantage in the end exactly because they challenge our understanding and haunt our imagination with a vision of heretofore unimagined possibilities rather than merely saddling us with rote reiteration of the shopworn patterns of the past.

Together, the authors in this volume probe a labyrinth of parables. The wit and wisdom of Billy Collins' advice to students regarding poetry applies equally to the prospective reader of this book—and to every fresh reading of Jesus' parables: be sure to bring your own mouse or whatever rodent you prefer to drop into the maze; then watch attentively as it probes its way out with persistence, agility, and aplomb.

Chapter One

Jesus' Parables and the Fiction of the Kingdom

Lane C. McGaughy

Matthew, Mark, Luke, Q, and the Gospel of Thomas tell us that Jesus was a skillful teacher whose way of communicating with his hearers was highly unusual, even novel: he composed fictional narratives and brief comparisons called parables. What are parables? C. H. Dodd in a book called *The Parables of the Kingdom* defines a parable as follows:

> At its simplest the parable is a metaphor or simile drawn from nature or common life, arresting the hearer by its vividness or strangeness, and leaving the mind in sufficient doubt about its precise application to tease it into active thought (p. 5).

The interpretation of Jesus' parables has become a major preoccupation of Gospel scholarship since the nineteenth-century attempt to anchor Christianity in an historically verifiable biography of Jesus proved impossible. The new quest of the twentieth century has thus turned to the words of Jesus in an attempt to relate the missionary preaching of the early disciples to the intention of Jesus' proclamation. In the Gospels,

The Fourth R 3,4 (1990), 8–11

the words of Jesus that are commonly recognized as being the
most authentic are the parables. Thus the attempt to recon-
struct the message of Jesus must take account of, if not begin
with, the synoptic parables.

A Short History of Parable Interpretation

From the first century through the nineteenth century the
parables were mainly interpreted as allegories. Early Christian
interpreters read the parables as allegories (1) because of the
prevailing worldview that equated reality with an invisible
supernatural realm and considered the sensible world a mere
shadow of the real, and (2) because of the widespread use of
allegory by the Alexandrian scholars to discover the non-literal, deeper meanings that lay behind the surface of Homer,
Hesiod and the Old Testament.

It was not until the nineteenth century, in the wake
of the modern scientific view of reality promoted by the
Enlightenment, that the allegorical interpretation of Jesus' parables was challenged by Adolf Jülicher. He argued in a mam-
moth 650–page work that the parables are example stories
that make a single point of the broadest possible application.
In light of the liberal attempt to conform the message of Jesus
to the ethical idealism of the late nineteenth century, Jülicher
usually interpreted this single point in moral terms.

Subsequent interpreters agreed with Jülicher that the
parables make one point. But they replaced Jülicher 's general
principle with a specific point related to the historical circumstances of Jesus' ministry. In the case of C. H. Dodd and
Joachim Jeremias, these historical circumstances are defined in
terms of Jesus' proclamation of the imminent arrival of God's
reign. In the words of Robert Funk, "Jülicher 's moral point
of broadest possible application" was replaced by Dodd and
Jeremias with an "eschatological point of particular historical
application."

Early twentieth-century interpreters from Jülicher to
Jeremias have, in general, rejected the traditional allegorical
interpretation by restricting the meaning of the parables to
a single point. Yet they have not escaped the "rationalizing"

approach of allegory, which assigns specific meanings to the parables. It does not matter whether that specific meaning refers to the present (Jülicher) or the past (Dodd, Jeremias). In either case, the power of the parabolic image is destroyed.

In the past three decades a new line of parable interpretation has emerged in America. This line views the parables as open-ended language events or, more precisely, as extended metaphors. Pioneers of the new view include Amos N. Wilder, Robert W. Funk, J. Dominic Crossan, Norman Perrin, Bernard B. Scott, and John R. Donahue. Why have scholars come to regard parables as metaphors?

The Problem of Language

As a teacher, Jesus faced an enormous problem. He wanted to proclaim the arrival of something totally new called "the Kingdom of God," but he could communicate this only through the old language and symbols of his religious tradition, Judaism. Why was this a problem? Common, everyday or discursive language can speak directly only about what we already know. The predicate of a normal sentence simply spells out what is already contained or implied in the subject. Consider the following declarative sentence:

       S   V   P
1. Superman / is / strong.

The subject (S), "Superman," has many characteristics. The predicate (P) selects one of these characteristics, "strong" (not "weak"), and attributes it to the subject. In mentioning Superman, however, we already know that one of his attributes is strength. Thus sentence 1 simply puts in words what we already know about him and provides no new information. Other examples of everyday sentences in which the predicate simply selects one of the subject's possible features are the following:

2. It is sunny today. (It could be raining.)
3. Larry wants to play softball. (He could take a walk.)
4. My house is clean. (It could be messy.)

In each of these sentences, the subject implies known alternatives; e.g., in 2 it could be sunny or rainy today. Sentence 2 thus selects one of those possibilities and states it as the predicate.

Metaphorical Language

The subject of Jesus' speech, the Kingdom of God, was absolutely novel. No one had experienced it before. There was no familiar language with which it could be directly described. He thus employed a different kind of language, parable, to speak about the Kingdom of God indirectly. Parables are examples of metaphorical language. In a metaphor, the predicate is not contained or implied in the subject. Compare the following sentence 5 with 1 above:

      S   V   P

5. Superman / is / a lion.

Superman has many characteristics—he is a man, he is strong, he is young, etc.—but he is not literally a lion. Sentence 5

The Sower

Luke 8:4–8

[4]Since a huge crowd was now gathering, and people were making their way to him from city after city, he told them such a parable as this: [5]"A sower went out to sow his seed; and while he was sowing, some seed fell along the path and was trampled under foot, and the birds of the sky ate it up. [6]Other seed fell on the rock; when it grew, it withered because it lacked moisture. [7]Still other seed fell among thorns; the thorns grew with it and choked it. [8]Other seed fell on fertile earth; and when it matured, it produced fruit a hundredfold." During his discourse, he would call out, "Whoever has two good ears should use them."

Translation from the *Scholars Version* (Polebridge Press)

is thus a figurative or metaphorical sentence in which two terms, "Superman" and "lion," are grammatically placed in the subject and predicate positions even though there is no direct connection between the two. The predicate of a metaphorical sentence, however, is able to illuminate the subject because the two terms share some quality in common. In this case, both Superman and a lion are symbols of strength, although they differ in most other ways. The quality of strength is thus the unstated middle term which enables sentence 5 to "work." But we cannot apply any other characteristics of a lion to Superman: he is not four-footed, he does not have a tail, etc.

Another example of a metaphorical sentence was created by the poet Christina Rosetti:

6. My love is like a red, red rose.

Although my experience of love for another person is not literally to be equated with a flower, the two terms share some feature—perhaps the beautiful feeling both evoke—that produces a new insight when heard for the first time.

The Parables of Jesus

Jesus constructed fictional stories and brief comparisons— there are some 65 parables in the Synoptic Gospels—to illuminate metaphorically the Kingdom of God. The formula he uses is:

S   V   P

The Kingdom of God / is / like a parable.

As a metaphor, the parable that occupies the predicate position does not directly define the Kingdom of God—we cannot identify the actors in the parables with God, Jesus, the Pharisees, or any other individuals or groups. Rather, Jesus suggests that the parable and the Kingdom of God share a middle term in common; there is something about the parable as a whole that is like the Kingdom of God.

Each parable begins with an event or image from daily life—none of the parables is about a specifically religious topic.

The Mustard Seed

Luke 13:18–20

[18]Then he would say, "What is the imperial rule of God like? To what should I compare it? [19]It is like a mustard seed which a man took and tossed into his garden. It grew and became a tree, and the birds of the sky roosted in its branches."

Translation from the *Scholars Version*

As a result, the original audience was able to identify with the starting point of the parable and affirm, "Yes, that's the way it is." Somewhere in the process of narrating the parable, however, Jesus introduces an unexpected development or excessive exaggeration that drives the initial realism of the parable to an "unrealistic" conclusion. This twist or strange element forced the original hearers to respond decisively to the parable: either they were so shocked by the twist that they rejected Jesus' teaching about the Kingdom of God or, having accepted the unusual conclusion of the parable, they found themselves entering into this novel reality that Jesus labeled Kingdom of God. Jesus' pedagogic strategy in constructing the narrative parables can be diagrammed as follows:

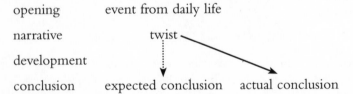

opening   event from daily life

narrative   twist

development

conclusion   expected conclusion   actual conclusion

Returning to our earlier discussion about the nature of language, we note how Jesus begins with ordinary, realistic language that describes some event from daily life or the natural world but transforms the story into a metaphor by means of an excessive exaggeration or hyperbolic element. Jesus was faced with the problem of revealing a new world—

The Leaven

Luke 13:20–21

²⁰He continued, "To what should I compare the imperial rule of God? ²¹It is like leaven which a woman took and concealed in three measures of flour until all of it was leavened."

Translation from the *Scholars Version*

one that had never entered language before—through an old language, the conceptual world of Judaism. His teaching strategy involved the use of metaphorical language—parables—which starts with the old world of the hearers but, by injecting a strange turn in the narrative or comparison, explodes that old language tradition so that the Kingdom of God might be glimpsed in the process. Since Jesus is metaphorically revealing a new reality, and not just correcting a wrong idea in Judaism, the parables do not make specific ethical or theological points. They are open-ended so that the hearer is drawn into the parable in such a way that the imagery of the parable reflects the entire world of the Kingdom of God: one either enters it on faith and conducts all his or her activities in light of this new horizon, or one is offended and retains his or her old way of viewing the world.

Chapter Two

How Jesus Took the Gist from Liturgist

Luke 18:10–14

Edward F. Beutner

E ven given the newfound modesty with which scholars are approaching textual data about Jesus of Nazareth, there remains the widespread consensus that he was a man who spoke and behaved in parables. To put an even finer point on it, he spoke in parables because of how he perceived the really real; and he behaved in parables because his gestures flowed in congruence with both his perception and his speech.

I do not like to say that Jesus "preached" or "acted" in parables simply because I do not imagine that he put on little plays or vignettes in order to prove or demonstrate some non-parabolic point. I say he spoke and behaved in parables because I take him as one who construes the real world as evocative, interrogative, parabolic: a world that is itself not fixed, not self-referential, not even self-contained; but forever fresh and gesturing.

Intimate attendance to the pulse and contours, hues and cries of so beguiling a world eventuates first in silence (the

The Fourth R 12,3 (1999), 3–6

start of wisdom, when one begins to wonder) and then in parabolic speech, at whose heart is metaphor.

The metaphor ingredient in parable is not metaphor-for-effect, but metaphor-as-epiphany: the most apt and least inadequate expression of a worldview that cannot be put in other words, but which will show itself at the periphery of sustained silent vision and in the cracks and crevices of engaging conversation.

From my reading of the gospels, it sounds to me as if Jesus conversed most frequently and unfailingly at table. He did it when he was dead serious and in high humor—states of mind which, I gather from his parables, he found to be extremely compatible. Examples abound, even in spite of the tattered, reworked state of his voice—which rarely thunders, but here and there will bob and weave and wink and nod its way through the gospel narratives.

But on your part and mine, eavesdroppers that we are, it takes a pair of ears attuned to irony, a heart aligned to radical reliance. Rigidity of jaw will deaden our eardrums to the allure of parable every time. But unclenched teeth, relaxed orifices, unbusied bodies—these equip us nicely for the sidelong assault of parable.

The historical Jesus looked not to history or its trends for validation, but to the particular and the irreducible everyday. He seemed to take with ultimate seriousness nothing other than the high regard of the nameless one whom for want of a better word he called father. Jesus gave himself over not to the astonishing theophanies of signs and wonders, but to the peripheral epiphanies in every human nook and cranny. His reigning metaphor for such endless goings-on was *basileia*: kingdom or empire.

What Jesus found all over the place was something that might well be called groundless mercy, which cannot be merely earned, but is of another world entirely. We are not likely to hear the voice of Jesus if we are hanging onto anything for dear life, least of all to life itself as we know and cherish it. We are more likely to hear his voice when we are simply hanging out, an activity the historical Jesus seemed inordinately fond of for a man of his age.

Hanging out is a somewhat freewheeling activity that tends to ignore social maps. Social maps are the constructs that every human culture, whether civil or religious, provides for its members; such maps and scripts operate in our minds, consciously or not, as a way of identifying and discriminating between "insiders" and "outsiders," between "us" and "them." Hanging out is socially unacceptable when it is seen to be in violation of the social boundaries established by our cultural, religious, political, and economic maps and scripts.[1]

The insouciance of Jesus regarding social maps and scripts was legendary. His disregard for rigid religious boundaries may help account for his ready reception among the irreverent "outsiders"; no doubt it is also what earned him the disdain of the religious "insiders." On more than one occasion these elitist leaders were quick to confront Jesus with the scandal he was causing.

Because he treated their solemn warnings as unworthy of a second thought, and especially because he unrepentantly continued his activities, their disdain hardened—in some cases into hatred, plotting, and foul play. Hand in glove with Roman power, the ultimate "insiders" saw to his execution outside the Holy City—the disposal of just one more expendable "outsider." Make what you will of his execution, his parables are anything but incidental:

> Here are these two characters going up to the temple to pray: the first a full-fledged Pharisee and the second a petty tax officer.
>
> The Pharisee stands there all to himself and makes his pointed prayer:
>
> "God, I am so grateful for my specialness . . . that I'm not numbered among the thieves and cheats and adulterers of this world, and especially not among the likes of that petty tax officer back there."
>
> "Every single week," the "upright" man continues, "I fast for two full days [instead of only one]; and from every-

---

1. For more on social maps, see Scott, *Hear Then the Parable*, 92–98; and for more on social scripts, see Herzog, *Parables as Subversive Speech*, 191–93.

thing I earn, I always donate my ten percent to charity."

Meanwhile the petty tax officer is standing off in a corner, and without even daring to look up to heaven [the gesture of prayer], he bangs himself on the breast and says, "O God show me some mercy, sinner that I am."

"Say what you will," Jesus added, "but I contend that this last fellow went back to his home [and family] reconciled—which is more than I'll say for that first man."

"This goes to show how self-promoters manage to disgrace themselves, and how the self-effacing end up saving face."—Luke 18:10–14, revised EFB

Now, there is a way to moralize this story—perhaps, in fact, a dozen ways. The Calvinist in us can moralize damned near everything, and the Calvinist dies hard. But something happens when we remove the self-protective filters from our ears and allow the parable to land inconclusively in our laps not as an argument, not as a moral certitude, but as a haunting interrogatory about the relocation of the sacred, or maybe even about the obliteration of the boundaries walling off the sacred from the secular, the so-called sinner from the self-appointed saint. The story challenges us as listeners to let it knock our socks off—usually through the shock of self-recognition. ("Anybody here with two good ears had better start to listen.") No longer can we afford to come away from this parable muttering the prayer, "Thank God I am not like this Pharisee."

Worse still, we can no longer pray, "Thank God I am not like those who thank God they are not like the Pharisee." If we take this story to the extreme as a morality tale, we are likely to reduce, little by little, the list of people whom in our hearts we thank God we are not like. Eventually we may drop even Hitler from our list, and will no longer even have a list. But the trap of parable returns: after all, the implicit prayer is still comparative: "I thank God I am not like those people who still have a list." When the weight of this text hits us, we are struck by the parable as parable— a trap from which there is no exit, no safe escape. To put it in non-parabolic terms

(always a diminishment) is to suggest that the parable is leaving no ground anywhere in the universe on which any human
being can stand justified. There is only Ungrounded Mercy,
and to seek or claim grounds of any kind is to miss the mercy.
(This is not to claim that the mercy misses us; it is only to
observe that we can stiff-arm the joy of it.)

Robert W. Funk, in *Language, Hermeneutic, and Word of God*,
claims that to undertake the interpretation of parables is to
learn eventually that the hermeneutical shoe is on the other
foot. The deepest discovery, if not the earliest, is that the parable ends up interpreting the reader, and not the other way
around. To leave room within our hearing for the assault of
this or any parable is to prepare ourselves for the unexpected.
It leaves us listeners strangely open to the routine disruption
of our most highly cherished certitudes, and naively willing to
reconsider our most deeply ingrained habits. When Jesus asked
us to have two good ears for this kind of thing, he might have
warned us that it also takes an uncommonly strong stomach.

Another major insight in Funk's book reconstrues the
"how" of parable interpretation. Funk's proposal, since shared
by Crossan, Scott, Donahue, and many others, is this: the language of metaphor cannot be translated into discursive propo-
sitions, but must be experienced first-hand; interpretation
of parables should take place, therefore, in parables. By way
of tapping that rich vein, it might be well to end with two
examples:

> One day in synagogue
> a rabbi and a cantor and a janitor
> were preparing for the Day of Atonement.
>
> The rabbi beat his breast and bowed his head
> and said aloud, "I am nothing, I am nothing."
>
> The cantor beat his breast and bowed his head
> and said aloud, "I am nothing, I am nothing."
>
> The janitor beat his breast and bowed his head
> and said aloud, "I am nothing, I am nothing."
>
> And the rabbi said to the cantor,
> "Look who thinks he's nothing."

Doxologies

Two men approached the holy place of prayer.
One man was grateful, but not grateful beyond words.

He rose the modest virtuoso: score in hand, flushed of
heart and cheek.

He prayed artful and emotive, even confident: the huge,
traditional fugue of gratitude and praise.
He breathed surprising fire for one his age into old
inspired time-worn syllables.
He crescendoed emphasis at every word which said
that God and God alone be blessed as all in all;
and through his art the secondary theme of strict
observance remained all but barely audible, and
consummately unstressed.

The other man forgot his psaltery upon the spot,
forgot there was a place of safety where he could stand
when the unfamiliar terror of prayer came over him.
Inert and crusted as the mud beneath his feet, he neither
fled nor stepped ahead.
He stood, eyes fixed upon the ground of his predicament,
shoulders bent against annihilation.

Jesus maybe mistook the tremble of his nether lip for a
whispered word ("mercy") but the truth is that the man
said no such thing.
He stood still and stared dumbstruck into the sickening
abyss between nothing and everything.

Jesus figured that God took the first man at his word
and probably was outwitted; and that the second man he
took for dead so into the snot of his nostrils he breathed
the breath of life.

Chapter Three

On the Road Again

The Leased Vineyard

Bernard Brandon Scott

J esus Seminars on the Road (JSORs) provide for a significant interaction between the fellows and associates of
the Jesus Seminar. Not only do we meet associates whose
acquaintance we have made in Santa Rosa at the fall and
spring meetings, but hundreds of others learn of the Seminar's
activities. Over the years I have taken part in a number of
these JSORs, and always to my great enjoyment.

Following good biblical precedent, Westar sends us out two
by two. So on April 4, 2003, Daryl Schmidt and I arrived at
Newport News, VA, and were greeted by the Reverend Liz
Brown of the UU Fellowship of the Peninsula, our hosts for
a JSOR program on the parables. Daryl is one of my favorite
partners (not to slight my other comrades in arms), and we
follow a similar outline each time, but with enough varia-
tion to keep it interesting for us. I enjoy working with Daryl
because I always learn something from him. What many students do not realize is that we teachers learn more from our
teaching than the students do!

The Fourth R 16,2 (2003), 9–15

The Widow

Friday night began with a discussion of what a parable is, using as an example a rabbinic parable about a widow with two sons and the Q/Thomas parable of the Leaven. Below is the parable of the Widow, which plays a role in the story that follows.

> There was once a poor woman who dwelt in the neighborhood of a landowner. Her two sons went out to gather gleanings, but the landowner did not let them take any. Their mother kept saying, "When will my sons come back from the field; perhaps I shall find that they have brought something to eat." And they kept saying: "When shall we go back to our mother, perhaps we shall discover that she has found something to eat." She found that they had nothing and they found that she had nothing to eat. So they laid their heads on their mother's lap and the three of them died in one day.

When it comes to Jesus' parables we are often deaf. Having heard them so often, we find it hard to really hear them. This parable offers a fresh hearing because we have never heard it. When the widow and her sons die, it comes as a real shock. We are not expecting this and feel it in our guts. We do not have to use our heads to think about what happened.

While I cannot prove it, I think the parable of the Widow is a female parable, representing women's wisdom. The shock of its conclusion provokes empathy on the audience's part. The parable offers no magic wand to make the situation right, but it does let women know that someone else knows their story. In times of tragedy a sense of solidarity is often liberating.

Like Jesus' parables, this one was preserved by a scribe who added commentary; in this case one who understood power issued a protest, calling on God to vindicate the poor:

> Said the Holy One, blessed be He: "Their very existence you take away from them! By your life! I shall make you, too, pay for it with your very existence!"

> And so indeed it says, Rob not the weak, because he is weak, neither crush the poor in the gate; for the Lord will plead their cause, and despoil of life those that despoil them (Prov 22:22–23). (*Fathers According to Rabbi Nathan*, p. 158).

Leased Vineyard

Daryl began Saturday morning with a discussion of how we get from the Gospels back to Jesus' parables, using the gospel of Mark as an example. We have done this a number of times and I always warn Daryl that this is going to bring up the parable of the Leased Vineyard (Mark 12:1–12). Parables appear in two sections of Mark: chapter four (the Sower and several others), and chapter 12 (the Leased Vineyard). I have worked on the Leased Vineyard for more than twenty years, and have never felt satisfied with my interpretation. I see the parts and the problems, but I cannot figure out how to put them all together. I warn the audience that we are moving into dangerous waters. Daryl quietly reassures me that this time he has it figured out. Always I have faith; always I have been disappointed.

There are four versions of this parable. Matthew and Luke offer rewrites of Mark's text, while the Gospel of Thomas provides a very different version.

Before the discovery of the Gospel of Thomas, the central debate about this parable concerned its authenticity: Did a genuine Jesus parable lie behind the synoptic versions, or was it simply a salvation history allegory?

In Mark the parable is part of Jesus' temple debate with the Jewish authorities: the story reveals God's plan of history, and the authorities understand that the parable is directed against them. This revelatory character of the parable runs counter to an earlier statement (Mark 4:11–12), which says that the purpose of parables is to conceal Jesus' meaning. But that's not the case here. The temple authorities understand that they are the wicked tenants, Jesus is the son, and the owner of the vineyard is God. Thus the parable allegorically encodes and reveals the ending of the gospel. Indeed, many scholars have argued that the story so perfectly recapitulates the gospel's plot that the parable could not be from Jesus, but must be a creation of the early church. Adolf Jülicher, the founder of modern parable criticism, championed such a view (2:406; see my *Re-Imagine the World*, 151, for Jülicher's significance).

Some, like Joachim Jeremias, whose work dominated the post-WWII discussion of parables, demurred. For him the

Mark 12:1–12	Matthew 21:33–45	Luke 20:9–20
Someone planted a vineyard, put a hedge around it, dug a winepress, built a tower, leased it out to some farmers, and went abroad.	There once was a landlord who planted a vineyard, put a hedge around it, dug a winepress in it, built a tower, leased it out to some farmers, and went abroad.	Someone planted a vineyard, leased it out to some farmers, and went abroad for an extended time.
2In due time he sent a slave to the farmers to collect his share of the vineyard's crop from them. 3But they grabbed him, beat him, and sent him away empty-handed.	34Now when it was about harvest time, he sent his slaves to the farmers to collect his crop. 35And the farmers grabbed his slaves, and one they beat and another they killed, and another they stoned.	10In due course he sent a slave to the farmers, so they could pay him his share of the vineyard's crop. But the farmers beat him and sent him away empty-handed.
4So once again he sent another slave to them, but they attacked him and abused him.	36Again he sent other slaves, more than the first group, and they did the same thing to them.	11He repeated his action by sending another slave; but they beat him up too, and humiliated him, and sent him away empty-handed.
5Then he sent another, and this one they killed; many others followed, some of whom they beat, others of whom they killed.		12And he sent yet a third slave; but they injured him and threw him out.
6He still had one more, a son who was the apple of his eye. This one he finally sent to them, with the thought, "They will show this son of mine some respect."	37Then finally he sent his son to them, with the thought, "They will show this son of mine some respect."	13Then the owner of the vineyard asked himself, "What should I do now? I know, I will send my son, the apple of my eye. Perhaps they will show him some respect."

7But those farmers said to one another, "This fellow's the heir! Come on, let's kill him and the inheritance will be ours!" 8So they grabbed him, and killed him, and threw him outside the vineyard.

9What will the owner of the vineyard do? He will come in person, and do away with those farmers, and give the vineyard to someone else.

10Haven't you read this scripture, "A stone that the builders rejected has ended up as the keystone. 11It was the Lord's doing and is something you admire"?

12[His opponents] kept looking for some opportunity to seize him, but they were still afraid of the crowd, since they realized that he had aimed the parable at them. So they left him there and went on their way.

38But when the farmers recognized the son they said to one an-other, "This fellow's the heir! Come on, let's kill him and we'll have his inheritance!" 39And they grabbed him, dragged him outside the vineyard, and killed him.

40When the owner of the vineyard comes, what will he do to those farmers then? 41They say to him, "He'll get rid of these wicked villains and lease the vineyard out to other farmers who will deliver their produce to him at the proper time."

42Jesus says to them, "Haven't you read in the scriptures, 'A stone that the builders rejected has ended up as the keystone. It was the Lord's doing and is something you admire'?

43Therefore I say to you, God's domain will be taken away from you and given to a people that bears its fruit."

45And when the ranking priests and Pharisees heard his parable, they realized that he was talking about them. They wanted to seize him, but were afraid of the crowds, because every-one regarded him as a prophet.

14But when the farmers recognized him, they talked it over, and concluded: "This fellow's the heir! Let's kill him so the inheritance will be ours!" 15So they dragged him outside the vineyard and killed him.

What will the owner of the vineyard do to them as a consequence? 16He will come in person, do away with those farmers, and give the vineyard to someone else. When they heard this, they said, "God forbid!"

17But [Jesus] looked them straight in the eye and said, "What can this scripture possibly mean: 'A stone that the builders rejected has ended up as the keystone'?

18Everyone who falls over that stone will be smashed to bits, and anyone on whom it falls will be crushed."

19The scholars and the ranking priests wanted to lay hands on him then and there, but they were afraid of the people, since they realized he had aimed this parable at them. 20So they kept him under surveillance, and sent spies, who feigned sincerity, so they could twist something he said and turn him over to the authority and jurisdiction of the governor.

parable did come from Jesus and Jesus was the son in the parable. Of course, he had to admit that in that case the reference would not be understood by anyone listening to the parable (77). Thus Jeremias's "solution" is no solution at all, but only reinforces the allegory.

The chart on page 24 indicates the parallels between the synoptics. Mark (column 1) is the source for Matthew (column 2) and Luke (column 3).

- The synoptic version has elaborated the vineyard by reference to Isaiah 5:2–3.
- The expected sending of three has moved in a variety of directions.
- The son is the apple of his father's eye (literally "beloved"), a clear reference to Jesus as God's only son.
- The son is either killed or thrown "outside" the vineyard, a reference to Jesus' crucifixion outside Jerusalem.
- Following the son's death, there is a demand for the father to seek vengeance and take the vineyard away from the killers. This supports Christian supersessionism.
- Finally, the quote from Psalm 118 about the building stone is an allegorical reference to Jesus' resurrection.

Clearly, the synoptics have constructed a thoroughgoing allegory of salvation history (for an extensive analysis of the allegory see my *Hear Then the Parable*, 245–48).

Gospel of Thomas

The discovery of the Gospel of Thomas completely changed the discussion of the parable. Compared to Mark, Thomas is clearly much compressed and simpler; that it follows the rule of three also speaks to its originality and antiquity. But it would be naïve to think that Thomas' version is without editing. Not only is the importance of knowing (vs 4) a repeated theme in Thomas, but knowing and violence are associated in the parable of the Assassin (Thom 68):

> Jesus said, The Father's kingdom is like a person who
> wanted to kill someone powerful. While still at home
> he drew his sword and thrust it into the wall to find out

whether his hand would go in. Then he killed the powerful one.

Indeed, the Assassin may give us a clue as to how Thomas understood the parable: The one who knows should act forcibly and boldly, even if scandalously.

And besides providing us a glimpse behind the synoptics, the discovery of Thomas confirmed that their version was an allegory, probably an elaboration by Mark to fit his gospel plot.

Ironically, one of Jeremias' chief competitors, the English scholar C. H. Dodd, had reconstructed a non-allegorical version of the parable of the wicked tenants from the synoptic allegory. His reconstruction was dismissed as merely hypothetical, but when the Gospel of Thomas was discovered, the similarity of Dodd's 1935 reconstruction to the Thomas version strikingly confirmed his effort. It further indicates that while hypothetical, our reconstructions are not arbitrary.

Conundrum

So while we might have confidence that the Thomas parable is close to the Jesus version, we are still left with the problem of what it means. Without the allegory, how does one make sense of the parable?

John Dominic Crossan, the co-Chair of the Jesus Seminar, took an early shot at solving this problem. Crossan saw the parable as a realistic picture of the violence that plagued first century Galilee:

> It is a deliberately shocking story of successful murder. The story is certainly possible and possibly actual in the Galilean turbulence of the period. It tells of some people who recognized their situation, saw their opportunity, and acted resolutely upon it. They glimpsed a way of getting full possession of the vineyard by murdering the only heir and, with murderous speed, they moved to accomplish their purpose (96).

The strength of Crossan's analysis is his focus on the parable's violence, an element we should not lose sight of. But however suggestive his reading may be, it is ultimately unconvincing for two reasons.

Thomas 65-66	Mark 12:1-12
A [...] person owned a vineyard and rented it to some farmers, so they could work it and he could collect its crop from them.	Someone planted a vineyard, put a hedge around it, dug a winepress, built a tower, leased it out to some farmers, and went abroad.
He sent his slave so the farmers would give him the vineyard's crop. They grabbed him, beat him, and almost killed him, and the slave returned and told his master. His master said, "Perhaps he didn't know them."	[2]In due time he sent a slave to the farmers to collect his share of the vineyard's crop from them. [3]But they grabbed him, beat him, and sent him away empty-handed.
He sent another slave, and the farmers beat that one as well.	[4]So once again he sent another slave to them, but they attacked him and abused him. [5]Then he sent another, and this one they killed; many others followed, some of whom they beat, others of whom they killed.
Then the master sent his son and said, "Perhaps they'll show my son some respect."	[6]He still had one more, a son who was the apple of his eye. This one he finally sent to them, with the thought, "They will show this son of mine some respect."
Because the farmers knew that he was the heir to the vineyard, they grabbed him and killed him. Anyone here with two ears had better listen!	[7]But those farmers said to one another, "This fellow's the heir! Come on, let's kill him and the inheritance will be ours!" [8]So they grabbed him, and killed him, and threw him outside the vineyard. [9]What will the owner of the vineyard do? He will come in person, and do away with those farmers, and give the vineyard to someone else.
[66]Jesus said, "Show me the stone that the builders rejected: that is the keystone."	[10]Haven't you read this scripture, "A stone that the builders rejected has ended up as the keystone. [11]It was the Lord's doing and is something you admire"?

1. Jesus' parables at times focus on violence but do not recommend it as a solution.
2. How do the servants think that by killing the heir, the vineyard will be theirs? The inheritance problem remains.

But neither am I particularly persuaded by my own analysis of the parable in *Hear Then the Parable*. Having criticized Crossan for ignoring the issue of inheritance, I attempted a solution: The tenants remark that the son is the heir and think that by killing him the vineyard will be theirs. They must be mad! But the craziness of this logic warrants the synoptic allegory that the father will come and destroy them—surely the proper conclusion. And if not the father, then other landowners who would have much to lose by allowing such an example to stand.

In oral cultures, I continued, the way one quotes is by using a word or phrase to conjure up the image invoked by the reference. For example, in the parable of the Leaven, three measures summons up the story in Genesis 18: when Yahweh appears in the guise of an angel to foretell the birth of Isaac, Sarah prepares cakes from three measures of flour. Or in the parable of the Mustard Seed, the reference to the birds making nest in the bush's shade invokes the great cedar of Lebanon, an image appropriate for a kingdom, in ironic contrast to the mustard plant. In the parable of the Widow, gleanings refers to the command of Leviticus: "When you reap the harvest of your land, you shall not reap to the very edges of your field, or gather the gleanings of your harvest. . . . you shall leave them for the poor and alien" (Leviticus 18:9–10).

I also noted that Jacob's inheritance is a primary symbol in Israel's self-understanding. The inheritance is ill-gotten, stolen from the rightful heir. Thus the inheritance comes to stand not for a benefit that is earned or rightful, but for Israel's having been chosen, elected to its special place among the nations. It is God's free gift to his people.

In this way I tried to move beyond Crossan and see the parable as a comment on Israel's efforts to reclaim its inheritance. The owner is a fool, the tenants are bandits, and both the messengers are beaten or murdered. To whom does the inheritance rightfully belong? The parable offers no answer. In the parable's plot, the kingdom fails and the inheritance is in doubt (*Hear Then the Parable*, 251–53).

In the end, I don't find my own analysis convincing. It comes too close to allegory and sounds too much like a puzzle. Yet I think the Jacob theme is probably somehow involved, and that Crossan pointed us in the right direction.

A Voice in the Audience

Now back to the JSOR in Newport News. Daryl was holding forth in yet one more effort to make sense of the parable and I remained unconvinced, kibitzing back and forth with him.

Then from the audience came a suggestion that broke the log jam. Elise Hansard remarked, "It's just like the parable of the Widow we heard last night. It makes the violence real and sickens you."

There it was—the comparison that enabled me to see how the parable worked. Crossan is partly right and I was partly right, but Elise Hansard had the real solution. The parable points out the horror and hopelessness of the situation. To reclaim the inheritance by violence will lead only to an unending cycle of violence.

Unlike Thomas, who understands the point to be that knowledge should lead to decisive action, Jesus' parable calls on us to feel the violence, then stop and think. Thus it coheres with the anti-apocalyptic theme that runs throughout Jesus' parables and sayings (see *Re-Imagine the World*, 124–28). In the Mustard Seed the plant does not become the great cedar of Lebanon, the appropriate metaphor for a kingdom; it is more like a weed. In the Seed and Harvest (Mark 4:26–29), the harvest belongs to a farmer who does not quite know what is going on. He does not observe the activity of God because he is asleep. But the last line of the parable quotes a passage in Joel about the end-time, apocalyptic war. "Prepare war, . . . Beat your plowshares into swords and your pruning forks into spears; . . . Put in the sickle, for the harvest is ripe" (Joel 3:9–13). When the farmer puts in his sickle the occasion is not the ultimate end-time war between nations, but the actions of a farmer who is simply bringing the harvest in.

Each of these parables echoes in oral quotation a theme from the Hebrew mythical tradition, but reverses the theme.

- Mustard plant reverses cedar of Lebanon
- Leaven reverses three measures
- Sleeping farmer reverses Joel's apocalyptic war
- The murdering tenants reverse Jacob's inheritance.

In the parable of the Leased Vineyard the violence of the parable warns the listener against attempting to reclaim the inheritance by violence. Jacob may have gotten away with deception, but this is different. This kingdom cannot be reclaimed by violence or the violence will be without end.

This JSOR was not extraordinary; rather it typifies what often happens. The audience was not just listening, sitting at the feet of the supposed masters. They were engaged. They were thinking, probing, asking questions, poking holes in our arguments. And most important, they were pushing the argument even further. Elise Hansard saw where the logic was going, made the connection to another piece of evidence, and advanced the cause of understanding Jesus' parables.

Once again, from the students the teachers have learned. That is why I keep doing Jesus Seminars on the Road.

Chapter Four

A Mercy Unextended

Matthew 18:23–34

Edward F. Beutner

L et me begin with the blunt assumption that Jesus of
Nazareth, no less than the rest of us, is finally betrayed in
his speech.

The religious imagination of Jesus—so evident, I think, in
the winks and nods and subtle color of this story—reverber-
ates unnervingly against the grain of our accustomed sense of
things, and speeds like either death or medicine directly to the
unguarded heart of much that we together treasure.

In this parable of Jesus nothing is at stake if our ears are
overtrained to protect us from the sidelong assault of irony.
But if our ears have never learned that deflective trick—or if
through joy or loss or grief or grace we have despaired of that
defense—then no less is at stake than the shape and contours
of the really Real. If the ears of our ears have been attuned to
an elusive God whom we admit we cannot name or locate,
then the parable is not a self-conscious teaching device at all,
but a shocking recognition story. A parable is a little like a joke,
but not an entirely innocent joke. Either we get it or we don't,

The Fourth R 12,5/6 (1999), 11–14

surprise and all; we get it especially if we hear it aimed ines-
capably at our exit strategies. As listeners we are in the batter's
box and the parable-teller approaches us like this:

PITCHER

His art is eccentricity, his aim
How not to hit the mark he seems to aim at,

His passion how to avoid the obvious,
His technique how to vary the avoidance.
The others throw to be comprehended. He

Throws to be a moment misunderstood.
Yet not too much. Not errant, arrant, wild,
But every seeming aberration willed.

Not to, yet still, still to communicate
Making the batter understand too late.

—Robert Francis

Jesus' stories may delight or dismay or frighten us as listeners because they are told not for the glorification of the obvious, but sometimes for the high surprise of irony over the
discovery of God's subtlety and ubiquity. Sometimes they are
aimed at our chagrin over the discovery that God's activity
happens in the places or moments we have been least likely
to anticipate. Jesus does not always deliver what our ears are
listening for. Listen for his voice; listen for the way he helps us
understand not that we don't ever understand anything at all,
but that we do indeed understand much of what we understand too late:

It should be obvious by now how the kingdom of
heaven compares with this one drug lord who decides to
settle up accounts with his dealers:
On day one this dealer is escorted in who, as it turns
out, is ten million dollars in arrears. Since the dealer
couldn't come up with the cash, the drug lord decides
to recoup his losses by arranging to have the dealer sold:
lock, stock and barrel; wife, children and home.
Faced with these prospects, the dealer gets down on
his knees, grovels and pleads with the drug lord, "Please,
please: if you will show patience with me, I promise I

will show up with everything I owe you, down to the
last penny." The drug lord (hardly famous for compassion) lets him off the hook, and even writes off the ten
million as a bad debt.

Having barely escaped [suffering only a loss of face],
that same dealer now has to go face-to-face with one
of his own underlings who owes him a hundred dollars. "Pay up, and pay up now," he cajoles, all the while
holding the man in a collar choke till he collapses. The
underling gasps and begs, "I promise I will pay you back;
just be patient with me."

But the dealer couldn't care less; no he turns his back
on the slacker and orders him to be pimp for his own
family until they earn enough to repay the debt.

Meanwhile, his fellow dealers got word of all these
goings-on, and everybody on the street got very jittery.
Some see to it that word of this gets delivered back to
the drug lord, a blow-by-blow account.

That did it. The drug lord calls the dealer on the car-
pet: "You scumbag," he lets him have it, "I wrote off your
whole debt after you begged me on your knees. Since
when do you think you can get away with not extending
the same 'consideration' I extended to you?" In fact, the
drug lord gets so enraged that he hands the dealer over to
his strong-arms, who [as we all know] have ways of per-
suading a dealer to pay back every last dime of his debt.

—Matthew 18:23–34, rev. EFB

This free-wheeling translation moves readers into the world
of drug-trafficking not for the sake of sounding up-to-date.
Rather, its purpose is to restore the emotional distance and
fear and disdain which Jesus' original listeners might well have
felt for the adversarial and crooked and alien and dangerous
world of the first century patronage system under which their
lives were being forcibly governed from afar. This is the world
about which the parable is ostensibly being told. Jesus' listeners felt oppressed and trapped by the ruthlessness and arrogant
"civility" of that world, and most felt unable to do anything
about it. Like peasants before and since, they were reduced to
playing along with its rules publicly; and for sheer relief, they

were reduced to making safe and sorry sport of it in their
private conversations.

Perhaps what Jesus did was take these private conversations and turn them into public discourse. By telling parables
Jesus was able to unmask the pretense of the bogus civility
of an oppressive world, and to reveal the fault lines shivering
beneath the surface of its moral posing. Just as in geometry
a parabola is not a straight line, so in storytelling a parable is
not a straight-line delivered to those whose vested interest
lies in maintaining and enforcing the status quo. A telling parable or two might well suggest immense disequilibrium in a
world whose "straightforward" narrative (laws, customs, myths)
assumes that all is orderly and fixed, and even sanctioned by
divine intent.

Jesus sees right through charades of that sort, and aims this
parable at the epicenter of such gangsterism, no matter where
it shows itself: whether in home, church, school, or state.

In the religious imagination of Jesus, God is not a gangster,
not a petty tyrant, not a king whose fragile ego needs to be
appeased or honored or groveled to. Nor in the parables of
Jesus is God represented by any such self-promoting stand-ins.
Despite the stories we hear over and over that cast God as the
"heavy," God is never the heavy in the stories of Jesus. God is
not the heavy in this parable either. But the parable does have
a heavy, and if we listen closely, we may understand (too late)
who the heavy is, and in whose general direction the parable is
heading.

Once we agree that the king is no one's stand-in, but
indeed appears as himself in the parable, then two things happen immediately within our hearing.

First, God is cast *outside* the parable, offstage, so to speak.
Once that happens, we are in a fresh position to understand
the irony of Jesus when he speaks of God's domain in terms of
a kingdom. Irony is the telling of a transparent lie—transparent
even to a child. Irony speaks a literal lie that does not under-
mine a truth, but underlines it. So if Jesus speaks ironically of
the activity of God as a kingdom, he may well mean "whatever else you think of, do not think of kingdom; think instead
of its exact opposite."

An everyday example of this use of irony occurred one time when I was eating at the table of my brother-in-law, a wise and thoroughly self-educated man. He had grown, I think, a bit weary of my expounding in academic jargon some scholarly point in response to a simple biblical question he had asked at table. He interrupted me just long enough to turn to my sister and say with a grin, "Ed sure has learned a lot about the Bible—but me, I graduated from the School of Hard Knocks." The academic in me may or may not catch the irony in the grin of his remark, but my sister knew exactly what he meant: he meant that, whatever else you might want to think of when you hear the word "school" in his phrase, you must not think of a school at all, but of its exact opposite.

Entertain with me the notion that in Jesus' phrase "kingdom of God," *kingdom* might have been served up to his original, king-beleaguered audience as such an irony.

Once God is cast outside the parable, a second thing happens within our hearing: we no longer find ourselves investing the king in the story with divine attributes; and we no longer feel impelled automatically to defend his every action as wise, reliable and irreversible. He takes his place alongside the rest of us mere mortals. Entertain with me the likelihood that the king in the parable is, like the rest of us, a mere mortal. Entertain too, the prospect that these petty kings were mortals much despised by the subjects over whom they ruled, whose land they had usurped. If such peasant nobodies comprised the bulk of Jesus' audience, then Jesus, through his irony, may have been turning topsy-turvy the notion of how authority is to be exercised in the "kingdom (think the opposite) of God."

This understanding of "lording it over" and that of "groundless mercy" cohere with the other parables of Jesus, and with his brief, memorable aphorisms alive in the oral tradition. This parable of Jesus does not confirm, but overturns, the behavior of the king. Jesus addresses his kingdom talk to the crowds and thus encourages them to uncouple their sense of God from their sense of craven fear of earthly overlords. In Jesus' time and place you can probably get away with this kind of talk privately; but what if the overlords overhear you, or what if you are reported, or what if you have simply decided to speak openly about subjects that are publicly taboo?

Consider for a moment the opposite prospect: that Jesus told this (and other parables) as a way of reinforcing and reconfirming the religious or political or social status quo. Such homespun stories about the arrival of the reign of God would have won him friends, not enemies, in high places. But that is not his story. Jesus' friends were for the most part from among the populace; his enemies came mostly from on high.

The historical Jesus was accused of sedition by perhaps a handful of the religious elites of Judea (who worked hand-in-glove with the occupying Romans). The historical Jesus was executed as a seditionist, a fate that the Roman government reserved for incorrigibles who didn't know enough to leave well enough alone.

I propose we read this parable of Jesus as an ironic commentary showing the starkest possible contrast between how self-serving humans govern among themselves, and how it is to be instead in the here-and-now kingdom (!) of God. In this reading, the contemptuous ruler is the heavy, and so is the snake-nest of indentured relationships that support his arrogance and pretense vis-à-vis all other human beings, whom he blithely regards as no more than an expendable supporting cast. Thus the irony of Jesus' referring to the domain of God as, of all things, a *kingdom*:

Whatever else God's "kingship" may or may not be like, it does not resemble the exercise of executive clemency as a kind of political expediency—however wise or praiseworthy—that can or will be withdrawn when it no longer serves the agenda of the monarch. In a word: Mercy is not mercy if you can find grounds for it. In other words, either mercy is unspeakable, or else we have to find another name for it.

That reading of the parable in its original setting may explain Jesus' popularity among the destitute and hard-pressed nobodies of his day; it may also help us understand his reputation as a troublemaker among the ruling elite. But why would we bother with such a parable today?

The parable today is aimed at us to be "a moment misunderstood." Too early and too soon we align ourselves with the world-view in which Jesus' story seems to be saying: mercy can be as calculated as anything else; you can switch it on or off as it pleases you; you can withhold it from anyone who offends you by seeming "undeserving." That is how it is. At the end of this parable, we sense that, despite the several tensions *during* the story, all is well again, and equilibrium has been restored.

Not so.

Too late we understand that the behavior of the drug lord is in *contrast* to the behavior that goes on in the heart of God. Too late we are hit by the shock of self-recognition. Too late we see the vision of the parabler: that while God extends groundless mercy to us, we have settled for a form of cold and controlled executive clemency upon those we regard as our inferiors (!) and are reduced to ingratiating behavior toward those we regard as our superiors (!).

Once we understand that we have understood too late, we are still in the batter's box of parable, which lets us see our situation as though for the first time. One of the things we have understood too late is that it is never too late to understand. In the religious imagination of Jesus of Nazareth, genuine religion is nothing like a board- or parlor-game. Instead, in the stories of Jesus, everything is at stake: it is the dust-unsettled world of parable, where life ain't over till it's overturned.

Chapter Five

The First
Will Be First

The Laborers in the Vineyard

Paul Verhoeven

I t is amazing that none of the commentaries on the parable of the Laborers in the Vineyard points out a crucial aspect of the narrative: that it tries to deceive us with a patently false statement in 20:10a: "Those hired first approached thinking they would receive more."

In 20:9 Matthew describes how the *eschatoi* (Greek for "last")—the workers hired at 5 PM—get paid first and receive a denarius. Then he suddenly jumps over to the payment of the *protoi* (Greek for "first")—those hired at 6 AM, and thus deliberately omits mentioning the payment of the workers-in-between, the ones who got hired at 3 PM, noon, and 9 AM. From verse 8 we know that they also got paid, in that order, after the *eschatoi*, and before the *protoi*.

If Matthew had done his job as a writer honestly he would have told us that the workers hired at 5 PM, noon, and 9 AM also got paid a denarius before he reported the same about the *protoi*. And then we would have realized that these *protoi*, after seeing what happened to all the others, could not have been

The Fourth R 16,3 (2004), 3–10

hoping that "they would receive more." They would by then be angry because they could have concluded only that they too would receive a denarius.

It's easy to accept that Matthew "cheats." After all, he frequently changes Mark to fit his theological and apologetic agenda. But it's not so easy to assume that Jesus was also a manipulative storyteller. The rest of his parables—as far as we can detect their original versions from the rewrites of the synoptics—display clarity, coherence, and internal logic. I do not believe that Jesus would have told his parable in the deceptive way Matthew dares to present it to us.

Another facet of Matthew's narrative is also disturbing: at the end of the day, at 6 PM, the owner of the vineyard orders his steward to pay the wages "starting with those hired last" (verse 8). This would have been against normal procedure. The owner would pay the *protoi* first and then would go down the line to the *eschatoi*. To force the laborers who had worked for twelve hours, who had worked through the heat of midday while, as the great scholar Adolf Jülicher put it, "they were scorched by the blistering southeast wind"—to force these men to stand at the end of the line to receive their pay, is cruel. They had to watch while all the others, who had worked fewer hours, were being paid the same wage: one denarius.

Some commentators have recognized the rude behavior of the owner, but soften it immediately by explaining that we shouldn't take this as an affront. It is just a literary device that Jesus used when he constructed this parable: by putting the *protoi* at the end of the line they could witness the generous reward accorded their comrades. If the *protoi* had been first in line for payment they would, according to Jülicher, "immediately have rushed home with their payment, and would only have heard later by hearsay that recently some workers got paid as much for one hour of work as others got for six or twelve hours." I don't believe that Jülicher's argument holds, and I'll come back to this later.

But even so, would Jesus have taken pleasure in constructing a narrative where the *protoi* are forced to the end of the line and are thus humiliated in front of the others? Only if he had felt that the owner was a real villain.

This has been argued recently (1994) by William Herzog, who writes:

> the *protoi* have been shamed. The landowner has aimed a deliberate insult at them, . . . he has told them that he values the day long effort in the scorching heat no more than the brief labor of the 11th-hour workers. He has shamed their labor.

In this Marxist reading of the parable, Herzog thinks that the insulting behavior of the owner is "a strategy for keeping the oppressed under control by humiliating and degrading them." I think Herzog's interpretation is ultimately wrong because he believes that Matthew's narrative corresponds to the original version of the parable as Jesus told it. I don't believe that to be true, and I'll indicate later what I think was the original. But Herzog is entirely correct on one point: if Jesus had told the parable as Matthew reports, it can be read only "as a codification of oppression" of the poor, the expendables. The landowner should then be seen as "a member of an oppressing elite class."

So we would have a parable with a big cheat in the narrative, and a vineyard owner who is a villain, whose "generosity" is nothing more than a method to divide the lower classes and humiliate them. Certainly not, we may hope, a figure that stands in for God.

Is this the last word? I believe not. To make my point I will again consider verse 8. This verse has been a problem to many commentators, some of whom have proposed omitting it, others reading it in a simplified way—for example, "Pay all the workers including the ones I hired last." The order of payment might not be essential. It is not what the *protoi* are upset about. They complain only that all are paid equally.

I therefore propose a simple change in the wording of the parable: omit "starting with the last up to the first" and read verse 8 simply as "When evening came the owner of the vineyard said, "Call the laborers and pay them their wages"; or even simpler, "When evening came the owner of the vineyard paid them their wages." Then the parable would unfold as follows. In natural order, the first in line to receive their

Matthew 20:1–15

For the Kingdom of Heaven is like a man, a householder, who went out early in the morning to hire laborers for his vineyard [2]Agreeing with the laboers for a denarius a day he sent them into his vineyard.

[3]And going out about 9 AM he saw others standing idle in the marketplace. [4]And to those he said, "You go into the vineyard too, and whatever is just, I'll give it to you. [5]And they went.

And again going out around noon and 3 PM, he did the same.

[6]And about 5 PM he found others standing and he says to them, "Why do you stand here idle all day?"

[7]They say to him, "Because nobody hired us."

He says to them, "You go too into the vineyard."

[8]When evening came the Lord of the vineyard said to his steward: "Call the laborers and pay the wage, beginning with last, up to the first."

[9]And when the ones who had been hired last came forward, they each received a denarius. [10]And when the ones came forward who had been hired first they expected to to receive more. And they each received a denarius too.

[11]And when they received it, they grumbled against the householder, saying, [12]"Those hired last only worked one hour and you made them equal to us who have borne the burden of the day and the heat."

[13]But he, answering one of them, said, "Friend, I do you no wrong; didn't you agree with me for a denarius? [14]Take what's yours and go. But I wish to give this last man the same as I gave you. [15]Am I not within my rights to do what I wish with what is mine? Or is your eye evil because I am good?"

Revised Parable

For the Kingdom of Heaven is like a man, a householder, who went out early in the morning to hire laborers for his vineyard. Agreeing with the laborers for a denarius a day, he sent them into his vineyard.

And going out about 9 AM he saw others standing idle in the marketplace. And to those he said, "You go into the vineyard too and whatever is just, I'll give it to you." And they went.

And again going out around noon and at 3 PM, he did the same.

And about 5 PM he found others standing and he says to them, "Why do you stand here idle all day?"

They say to him, "Because nobody hired us."

He says to them, "You go too into the vineyard."

When evening came the master of the vineyard paid them their their wages.

And those hired at 6 AM came forward and received one denarius each. But when the ones hired at 9 AM came forward, they also received a denarius. And they were amazed.

And the workers who began at noon and those hired at 3 PM came forward, and they each received a denarius. Even the workers hired at 5 PM, the ones that had worked only one hour, received a denarius.

Then the laborers who were hired first grumbled against the householder, saying: "Those hired last only worked one hour, and you made them equal to us who have borne the burden of the day and the heat."

But he, answering one of them, said: "Friend, I do you no wrong, didn't you agree with me for a denarius? Take what is yours and go. But I wish to give this last man the same, as I gave you. Am I not within my rights to do as I wish with what is mine? Or is your eye evil because I am good?"

wages would be the *protoi*, the workers hired at 6 AM. They
receive a denarius, as agreed. Then those hired at 9 AM get
paid; they also receive a denarius. Now the narrative starts to
intrigue us. What's happening? What is this owner doing? Then
the workers who began at noon arrive and they also get a
denarius. Now we, and Jesus' audience, are really amazed. This
is unheard of! And it gets even stranger: the workers hired at
3 PM and eventually even the *eschatoi*, the laborers who worked
for only one hour, in the cool air of the late afternoon, they
too get that denarius! This is perplexing. The audience is
baffled. This goes against all normal, decent behavior. That's the
kingdom of God!

- With this order of payment there would be a real buildup,
  an escalation of outrageous behavior, which corresponds
  to a similar build-up in the parables of the Merciful
  Samaritan and the Prodigal Son.
- The Samaritan bandaged and attended to the wounds of
  the victim, put him on his animal and brought him to an
  inn, gave the innkeeper two silver coins to look after the
  victim, and even promised to pay all further costs.
- In the Prodigal Son we also find five distinct acts of grace:
  the father runs out of the house to embrace and kiss his
  son, gets him the best robe, puts a ring on his finger and
  sandals on his feet, and finally slaughters the fattened calf
  for a feast to celebrate the son's return.

In my version the owner is no longer a cruel man who
seems to take pleasure in the degradation of the *protoi*. The
narrative is no longer deceptive. The careful and slow buildup
in verses 1–7 is mirrored by a similarly elegant buildup after
verse 8. And Matthew's clumsy short cut, where the narrative is suddenly reduced to a simple plot point without any
emotional resonance (apart from the grumbling of the *protoi*),
is avoided and replaced by the emotion Jesus' audience would
have felt as they saw a glimpse of the kingdom of God.

Jülicher's argument that this (new) order of payment would
prevent the *protoi* from hearing about the generosity of the
owner because they would "have rushed home" is artificial.
Jülicher brought it up mainly to provide some reason for

the unrealistic order that Matthew presents. It's also doubtful that an audience listening to the parable, in the version I
just presented, would immediately think that the *protoi* would
rush home. Think about it: what would happen immediately
after the *protoi* are paid? The moment the first of those hired
at 9 AM would have received his denarius—a couple of seconds after the last of the *protoi* got his—the astonishment
would spread. We can easily imagine one of those hired at
9 AM announcing, "Guys! Look at me. I got a whole denarius!
Wow!" No one would leave now. They would all be transfixed,
like Jesus' audience: what's happening here; where is this story
going?

Why would Matthew have changed the original order? The
solution can be found in the way he sandwiched his parable
between 19:31 ("Many of the first will be last, and of the last
many will be first") and 20:16 ("The last will be first and the
first last"). Most commentators agree that these sayings were
originally not attached to the parable, but were free floating,
as is still the case in Mark 10:31. In Luke 13:30 the saying
appears in a completely different context.

Matthew must have felt a strong need to attach these verses
to his parable (we'll return to the reason for this below). To
achieve this goal he first identified the first/last of Mark 10:31
with the workers who started at 6 AM/the ones who started
at 5 PM; but then later he also identified them as the workers
who were first in line for payment and those last in line. This
is a most arbitrary and superficial interpretation of what Jesus
must have meant by the Markan logion. To make this caricature work Matthew had to change the order of payment, that
is, start with the last so that those "hired first" would become
the "last in line." Otherwise those hired at 6 AM would still be
first in line!

If my reconstruction is correct, Matthew was willing to sacrifice the wonderful buildup that Jesus had constructed in the
second part of the parable. Matthew seems not to have cared
for the emotion that Jesus wanted to awaken in his audience.
Neither did Matthew understand that for listeners a buildup
is necessary, because it gives an audience time to realize what's
going on, it gives them time to let their emotions rise to the

surface, as everyone knows who works with the rules of drama (always a process in time) or the rules of musical composition. All the great arias of Mozart need time to be played out, and in them there is as much kingdom of God as in Jesus' parables. In both we can feel the kingdom of God "come alive."

Matthew was already a victim of the thinking of the early church that had forgotten about the reality of the kingdom of God and replaced it conveniently with the mythological lie of Jesus' resurrection. So after verse 8 Matthew "cut to the chase," as they say in Hollywood. By changing the order he compressed the emotional buildup Jesus had created into a simple plot point, as verse 9 makes almost fully and immediately clear. He then rushes forward into the narrative to emphasize the grumbling *protoi*, whom he probably identified with those Jews who opposed the young "Christian" church: that is, the Pharisees *et al.*

Why did Matthew force the saying in Mark 10:31 on this parable in such a destructive way? Jülicher makes some interesting observations about Matthew's theological agenda here. He points out that the parable is introduced by 19:30, which in the context of chapter 19 can mean only that

> "what will bring certain persons to the highest honor
> will cause others to take their deepest fall. . . . The Day of
> your Reward will be to others the Day of Eternal Doom.

In this way Matthew made 19:30 into an eschatological statement. And in my opinion, that's the interpretation he wanted to force on the parable too! The first should become the last: the men of Israel who thought of themselves as being the real representatives of God—the Temple authorities, the Sadducees, and the Pharisees—will on the Day of Reckoning (the Second Coming of Christ) all be doomed forever. Matthew wants to use the parable to announce to the leaders of the Jewish nation that their high positions will be taken away from them and given to the last, the poor, the insignificant (in short, the Matthean community of course); and they, the first of the past, will be expelled into utter darkness. Religious priority is subordinated to, drowned out by, mundane political forces: this is Matthew's own eschatological perspective. Or in Jülicher's words,

Under Matthew's hands this parable, this Gospel in a nutshell, that speaks only about the generosity of God, became a bitter indictment of the *protoi*, who count on a reward, but who are terribly wrong.

Through the centuries many scholars have identified the owner as a God figure. That seems unwarranted. Not only do the anthropomorphic actions of the owner go against it, but the parable is about God's kingdom, not about God. The parable is clearly a response to a question Jesus' audience might have asked regularly: what is this Kingdom of God like? Not: what is God like!

As in the case of the father in the Prodigal Son and the Samaritan, it might be preferable to see these figures as human beings. Their behavior should be seen as representing human behavior in God's kingdom, after the Spirit has been spread out as Joel prophesied: "I will pour out my spirit on all flesh." In the kingdom of God we will behave like the father of the Prodigal Son, like the merciful Samaritan, like this "owner of a vineyard."

It's quite possible that the original parable, in the form I have proposed, ended with the payment of the *eschatoi*. The Merciful Samaritan also ends immediately after the five acts of grace, and many commentators feel that the Prodigal Son ended with Luke 15:24, directly after the father has bestowed on his son an equal number of acts of grace. In all three parables Jesus would have sought to express his vision of the kingdom of God. More precisely, through his narrative Jesus would lead his audience into the Kingdom of God and they would feel a corresponding emotion. The breaking down of conventional wisdom, the tearing apart of social barriers, the display of unconditional love for the righteous and sinners alike, this "rupture" of reality as we know it, would evoke for Jesus' audience, if only for a brief moment, the breaking-in of God's kingdom.

There is however the possibility that material in Matt 20:12–15 was added to the original parable by Jesus himself, when, later in his ministry, he encountered growing adversity. If Jesus' behavior towards "sinners," especially in his open table community with its full acceptance of everyone, caused a lot of "grumbling," then this might have inspired Jesus to add a short second part to this parable, as he probably did to the Prodigal Son in the verses describing the reaction of the older son. When the *protoi* complained that they had been made "equal" to the other laborers who had worked less, the owner says, "Friend, I do not wrong you; you did agree for a denarius didn't you? Is your eye evil because I'm good?"

We should imagine this as part of a dispute with a priest, Levite, or scribe, where Jesus says: "When I keep company with 'sinners', I'm not doing you any harm, am I? You're doing your God-given part, and I'm doing mine. Are you angry because I'm good to these people?"

On the Laborers in the Vineyard

Paul Verhoeven
&
Robert J. Miller

April 2, 2003
Dear Paul,

I think you're on to something. I agree fully with your three major theses.

1. The story cheats by skipping directly from the workers paid first to those paid last. That is the only way to have the last workers be surprised at the outcome. The present story is simply not realistic and an audience would not let an oral storyteller get away with this.

2. The story is greatly improved by: i) reversing the order of the payout, and ii) narrating the payment to all the groups of workers, not just the first and the last.

3. The present narrative can be explained as Matthew's revision, which he makes in order to illustrate "the first will be last and the last first," a saying he uses as the framework for the parable.

Your analysis makes a significant contribution to the understanding of this parable. As with many important discoveries, one wonders why no one has pointed these things out before. Perhaps it's because most scholars are looking for religious meanings, gospel redactions, etc., while you are more alert to the narrative dynamics of the parable. For whatever reason, you've made a breakthrough here.

You've persuaded me that Matthew's version is not the original. However, whether Jesus told the parable in the form that you propose can never be more than speculation or wishful thinking. But so is a lot of Jesus scholarship. That's why we voted!

I hope that you put the parable in the movie in the version that you propose. Most viewers won't even know that your version differs from Matthew's! What you've done with this parable is to "help" the tradition to tell a better story—which is exactly what Matthew and Mark and Luke thought they were doing.

I want to focus on a feature of the story that you didn't discuss: the fact that the landowner goes back to the square several times to find more workers. Why didn't he simply hire everyone he needed at the start? Audiences would assume that he does this because he knows he can find unemployed workers any time of the day, and so he can go back and hire them for a partial day's wage (which is what everyone in the story assumes will be the case, so it must have been a customary arrangement). He goes back to the square throughout the day because he doesn't want to hire more than absolutely necessary at the full day's rate. He is thus minimizing his labor costs by exploiting a surplus supply of day labor: saving money by taking advantage of other people's misery.

The shock in the parable is not primarily that the owner pays all the workers the same. The major shock, and one that certainly offended much of Jesus' audience, is that a wealthy landowner is *not* exploiting his workers. A generous landowner is as much an oxymoron as a compassionate Samaritan.

April 7
Dear Bob,

I am aware of the point of view that sees the owner as an exploiter, but I believe it represents an internal contradiction.

You believe that in the first part of the parable the owner behaves in an exploitative way. But later he turns out to be a generous man! That means that he was a generous man from the beginning, so why would he use this "saving-money-by-taking-advantage" trick? His behavior as a real human being can be consistent only if he behaved as if he were a mean guy. Do you really think that's what Jesus meant?

There are only two possibilities for interpreting Jesus' intention: the owner was good, or the owner was bad. If Jesus meant him to be bad, you are back to an interpretation where the owner wants to humiliate the "first," a view that reflects Matthew's theological agenda. But the owner cannot be good *and* bad. In my opinion Jesus would not sacrifice consistency of character to plot construction. By the way, it nowhere says that the owner is "rich," unless we start with the understanding that every "owner" is rich. But why then, in the parable of the unjust steward, are we informed explicitly in the first verse that this "owner" *is* rich? The fact that this owner goes to the market himself (instead of sending his steward) might indicate that he is not rich at all.

April 8
Dear Paul,

You raise two questions: is the owner really rich? and is he good or bad?

1. The parable nowhere says the owner is rich. It doesn't have to. Anyone who owns so many grapes that his own family cannot harvest them, and anyone who has a steward (a full-time salaried assistant) is rich by the standards of that day. (If we read of someone today who gets around town in a limousine we know that he is rich, even if it doesn't say so explicitly.)

2. Is the guy good or bad? That is a true puzzle of this story, and I don't know exactly how to answer it. His generosity is evident in his wages. His retort to the laborer at the end of the parable shows him publicly shaming the worker, which seems mean-spirited. As for his making four trips to the square to hire workers throughout the day, what can it be except what I propose? (That's a real question, not a rhetorical one.) I don't know how to make his hiring practice consistent with his wage policy. It's clear that he doesn't hire everyone available in the morning and then come back to see if someone

else who needs work has shown up late for hiring; those who are hired last explain that they have been waiting around all day to be hired. This is even more puzzling because it seems to imply that the owner passed over these guys in his first three visits to the square.

There is more that is puzzling. Why does he go himself to do the hiring instead of sending his steward? (I don't take that as an indication that he is not rich.) And why does he lower himself to argue with the complaining worker, since it was the steward's job to deal with the workmen? That kind of verbal engagement between people of different social classes would be extremely unusual. Workers would be expected to communicate with the steward, not the owner.

April 8
Dear Bob,

The steward is not necessary for the story if the verse that Matthew invented, 20:9b, is eliminated. The father of James and John employed "hired hands": are they then *rich*? And my earlier question remains unanswered: why is the word "rich" applied to the man in the parable of the Unjust Steward? In general I have a problem interpreting the parables in "Marxist" terms, of exploitation of the masses etc., because I don't believe that people at that time could think that way. As to why the owner went back to the market five times, I suppose he must have realized that as the day went on he needed more workers to finish the job by 6 PM (for whatever reason— weather? delivery to customer?).

April 9
Dear Paul,

Is the owner rich? If he employs a couple of hired hands, probably not. If he has a steward and needs dozens of day laborers to bring in his harvest, then he certainly is. Since the parable doesn't give any solid information, it's up to us to make a guess. I'm still convinced that at the start of the story Jesus' audience would feel hostile toward the owner.

You don't believe that he's trying to get by on the cheap, because that would be inconsistent with your judgment about his moral character, although you have no other explanation for his unusual hiring behavior. Fair enough, but others will fill in the blanks differently. I don't think Jesus' audience would have looked favorably on his hiring practice, unless they knew ahead of time that he was a generous guy.

Marxism has nothing to do with my approach. People at the bottom (such as day laborers) can figure out that their precarious situation has something to do with the economic behavior of people at the top without ever having heard of Marx. Amos, Isaiah, Micah, et al. express moral outrage at the oppression of the poor, and there's nothing Marxist about that. It comes from Torah.

I want to propose a new way of looking at the owner's character. It requires some filling in, as so many of the parables do, so it depends on how plausible it will sound to you. Assume that the owner is rich and trying to get by on the cheap. (These are surely assumptions Jesus' audience would bring to the beginning of the story.) But then something happens to the owner. As he goes back time and again, he is touched by the despair of the guys he hires. When they line up to be paid, he again sees their situation (badly clothed, hungry, sickly?) and is stirred to compassion. Against everyone's expectations, including his own, he directs the steward to pay them all the same. The steward protests that this will cost him more than it should, perhaps more than he will get for the grapes they picked. He tells the steward, "It's my money and I can do with it whatever I want." (I like that last bit because it aims the owner's retort at the practical steward, rather than at the envious workers.)

What do you think?

April 9
Dear Bob,

In the sixties I often went to a house owned by the parents of my best friend. It was their holiday home and it was located in the Massif Central in France. The neighbor there was a farmer. I can assure you he was not rich, for the ground in that area is not very fertile. But he had a vineyard, not very big. Normally he and his family took care of that, but when the grapes had to be picked, he hired other people from the small (and also poor) village nearby. I can also assure you that this was a nice man.

If the steward weren't part of the story, like I proposed, then the situation of my French farmer would be quite like the one of Jesus' parable. The steward is necessary only to execute the very strange order, "Start to pay the workers who came last to the vineyard first, etc." If that order was never given then the order of payment wouldn't be a point, the steward wouldn't be part of the narrative, and only the equal amount paid to all the workers would stand out. Anyhow, it is weird that the owner (if he really *has* a steward) goes to the market to hire, is present when the payment takes place; and even starts a discussion with the workers. Everything is much more believable (for me!) if the owner does *not* have a steward, so that this cannot be used as argument to prove that he is rich.

I'm not sure at all that poor peasants would have insight in the economic situation of the upper classes. I don't think that peasants would understand the workings of the economy; I don't think they would know that something called "the economy" exists! It took us nearly 1900 years, after Jesus, to start seeing this. And yes, it was Marx and Engels who laid bare the machinations of capitalism. But doesn't it feel like an anachronism when this perspective is applied? Perhaps I underestimate Jewish peasants of 2000 years ago.

That the owner would change his mind during the day is quite possible, although I'm not sure that Jesus meant that. I will have to think about it.

April 10
Dear Paul,

Two final thoughts.

On the issue of economic awareness among peasants: Of course they wouldn't understand a concept like "the economy." They wouldn't understand the concept "religion" or "ethics" either. All those words are our modern abstractions. But imagine a peasant who used to own a small family farm but who lost it due to back taxes, and now gets hired (maybe) a few days a week to work on that same land for its new owner:

would that peasant understand that he had been exploited by forces infinitely more powerful than himself? Of course he would. I'm not referring to peasants having *theories* about the economy. They didn't have *theories* about farming, but they knew what worked and what didn't. They also knew when justice was present in situations like the payment of wages. And if they knew some of the Torah and the Prophets, they knew that God was against those power arrangements that enriched the powerful at the expense of those at the bottom.

On the "rich" question. I now see that the question of whether he was rich or how rich he was is secondary. What is at stake for me is how Jesus' audience is predisposed toward him as the parable begins. If he is rich, they won't like him, and this makes the surprise and shock of the parable work more effectively. If he is an average guy who just needs a few extra hands a couple of days each season, then the audience probably sees him more like themselves, and will tend to be sympathetic, in which case the discovery that he acts generously is much less of a surprise. Perhaps the key question is whether Jesus' audience starts the story identifying more with the owner or with the workers. My bet is with the workers.

Chapter Six

Comedy with a Tragic Turn

The Dishonest Manager

Edward F. Beutner

There was this powerful rich man whose financial
manager had been accused of squandering his
master's property. So he called him in and announced,
"What's this I hear about your management and as for
you, consider your job terminated."

So the financial manager frets to himself. "What am I
supposed to do now? My master is firing me summarily.
I'm not qualified to go out and dig ditches and I'm too
ashamed to live as a beggar." Suddenly he thinks, "I've
got it! I'll figure how to open some doors for myself
when I'm removed from my management position."

So he called in each of his master's debtors. He said to
the first one, "How much do you owe the old miser?"

The man replied, "Five hundred gallons of olive oil."

So he said to him, "Here's your invoice; sit down right
now and let's make it two hundred and fifty."

Then he turned to another debtor, "And you–how
much are you in arrears?"

He said, "A thousand bushels of wheat."

The Fourth R 16,2 (2004), 16–18

He says back to him, "Here, take your invoice and make it, say, eight hundred."

And the rich master heaped praise on his dishonest manager for his [new-found] shrewdness in the conduct of affairs ["under the table"].

So do [you really think that] the children of this world exhibit better sense in dealing with their own kind than do the children of light? Or [do you honestly think I'm suggesting] that you ought to make use of your ill-gotten gain to establish ties for yourselves, ties that will pull you up into eternal dwelling places when the bottom falls out?

—Luke 16:1–13, adapted EFB

Here is a parable that perhaps only Jesus can unlock for us. After all, it is his religious imagination that produced this story about a rich landowner and his financial manager. God knows that everyone from Luke (who first handed it along in writing) to this week's homilist has stumbled in the effort to "get it right."

Like Jesus' story about the eleventh-hour workers in the vineyard (Matt 20:1–15) who get paid the same as those who "bore the heat of the day," this parable arrives as a strange story, one for which there does not seem to be a satisfactory explanation. A lot like life, sometimes.

That may be where we have to begin with this (and all of) Jesus' parables. Like life, they do not arrive complete with solutions; they just stare us in the face and say, "This is how it is; make what you will of it." And every now and then Jesus adds, "If you have ears for this kind of thing, then be sure to hear it." Sometimes I wonder if he shouldn't have replaced "ears" with "stomach."

Sometimes we need uncommon stomach for that in life which we cannot "get right." This parable may be about something that we don't expect Jesus to be talking about. It may be about the infectiousness of corruption, with the emphasis on infectiousness.

In that respect it reminds me of the brief and pungent parable Jesus tells (Luke 13:18–19) about the woman who tries to smuggle in a little leaven (a pervasive symbol of corruption) by "hiding" it in a heap of dough–a scene right out of the Three Stooges. But anyway, to Jesus' way of thinking, the kingdom– or activity–of God does not exclude the comic.

There is, of course, a serious side to every comedy; but it is a side best left unspoken, best left to the imagination of the audience to make the connection between the comedy that disarmed them and the seriousness of what the comedy is pointing to or nudging us in the direction of.

It is not impossible, I think, to try this parable on as comedy —a kind of Keystone Cops routine, with all due respect; and I mean respect in the sense of a second, more protracted look.

The owner calls the manager to task and decides to dismiss him on the basis of rumor alone, absent any evidence ("What is this I hear about you?").

"Uh-oh," says the audience (which is not likely to identify with either the manager or the owner, since this kind of action takes place "over its head," you might say–among those who govern ruthlessly from afar rather than those who are governed without either consultation or consent).

Here, I think, would be a typical reaction to the story if Jesus is telling it to Palestinian or Galilean peasants of the first century: Jesus is telling a story about palace intrigue, and it has nothing to do with us at first blush, so we can sit and poke fun at those whose business it is to keep their place in the pecking order, and we can watch them bumble through, losing their self-respect in the process.

Even today, comedy is made of such stuff. Think of "Fawlty Towers" from the BBC, or of "Bless Me Father." Think of earlier (alas!) American films, in which those who aspire to be "upper class" are lampooned by movies starring Laurel and Hardy, Abbot and Costello, or the Bowery Boys; the list goes on.

Back to the parable: The rich man (CEO) is not so concerned about the truth of things (about which he never bothers to ask) as he is concerned about impressions. What will people think? The financial manager (CFO) is not interested in the truth of things either, but in how he will out-fox the CEO, who has pretty well decided to fire him.

(The audience still does not know whether or not the financial manager has actually squandered the owner's property or not, and that question—which ought to matter—gets lost in all the maneuvering which follows.)

Abruptly the scene shifts to the manager, who is suddenly very busy manipulating people who owe debts to the owner. He asks them what they owe the owner, then generously helps them to reduce their debts. The debtors do not know why he is being so generous to them, but the audience knows that he is hoping to stay in their good graces upon his dismissal. He does this for a reason that the audience should find highly entertaining: "To dig I am not able, to beg I am ashamed." This confirms their stereotype of a middle bureaucrat, whose job they view as a useless shuffling of papers.

When the owner eventually learns this, he compliments the manager. Honor, you might call it, among thieves. Picture it as a cartoon from the New Yorker. Boss to employee: "I'm afraid I have to admire your initiative, Hornsby."

All I see in this parable is that both the owner and the manager are worse off than when the story started. The owner is worse off because he has lost interest in the truth of things, if indeed he ever had it to begin with. And he ends up praising the manager, in whom he begins to see a mirror image of his own ingenuity; perhaps he's finally found a "worthy" protégé.

The manager is worse off, because he ends up being praised by one whose praise is tainted at best. It's like being honored by the Ku Klux Klan or the Aryan Nation: "No thanks" is what you and I might think, just as it might very well be what Jesus' original audience is thinking.

The owner and the manager are more alike than unalike; neither is living a simple, direct life, but both are caught in lives of intrigue that get neither of them anywhere worthwhile. They are tragic figures, presented in a comic piece. The comedy of it helps us distance them from ourselves long enough for a good laugh.

After the good laugh, we may now and again have moments of insight when we see ourselves capable of the same inanity which we laughed (to scorn) in them. "How unlike them we are" may some day turn to "How like them I have been; I must change my ways!" The parable functions as parable only if and when the laugh arrives at our own expense.

It may be how the mind of Jesus works: His "Thank God I am not like the Publican!" sooner or later starts to sound more and more like "Thank God I'm not like the Pharisee!" And that is when and how the parable traps us in the unadmitted middle of our complacency.

The exit from the trap comes, if at all, when we can laugh at our recognized selves in the same way that we were willing to laugh at our unrecognized selves. It is comedy come as extrication, or extrication come as comedy, whichever you prefer. Either way, it bears the earmarks of puzzlement, surprise, eccentricity, and irony—all of which are well-attested characteristics of the rhetorical strategy of Jesus and all of which, in our best unguarded moods and moments, we associate with grace.

Chapter Seven

The Pearl, the Treasure, the Fool, and the Cross

Robert J. Miller

The Overpriced Pearl

T he kingdom of heaven is like some merchant looking for beautiful pearls. When he finds one priceless pearl, he sells everything he owns and buys it. (Matt
13:45–46)

In all the gospels, this parable is the only one about an
object that is not native to Jesus' homeland. Jesus' listeners
knew what pearls were, but few if any of them had actually
seen one. For them, pearls were objects of fantasy; owning
even one pearl marked you as a member of the wealthy class.
In the imagination of Jesus' audience, pearls were symbols for
things of the utmost value. "Don't throw your pearls to pigs"
(Matt 7:6) needed no explanation; the contrast between what
is precious and beautiful on the one hand and those who are
disgusting and unappreciative on the other says it all. Ancient
authors often used pearls to describe something indescribably
beautiful. In imagining the heavenly Jerusalem, the Book of
Revelation conjures up a vision of pearls and gold of unearthly
size and purity: "The twelve gates were twelve pearls, each of

The Fourth R 18,6 (2005), 3–10

the gates made of a single pearl, and the street of the city was pure gold, transparent as glass" (Rev 21:21).

Jesus counted on his listeners to identify with the merchant in the parable, even though the character was in a higher social class than most everyone in his audience. For the folks who listened to Jesus, coming across a pearl would be too good to be true, a once in a lifetime opportunity. They would grasp the merchant's need to seize the moment and do whatever was necessary not to let the pearl slip away.

The merchant rises to the occasion with amazing single-mindedness. He is determined to obtain the pearl. He does not waver in his resolve and does not flinch at the cost. When he sees the pearl, he knows that this is what he's been waiting for and he believes it is worth whatever it takes. He liquidates his property ("everything he owns") and buys the object of his longing. (We can note that the pearl is subjectively but not literally "priceless"—if it were, the merchant would not have been able to purchase it.)

Jesus says that all of this is like the kingdom of God. So far, it seems clear. God's kingdom is worth anything and every-thing, and we must be prepared to commit ourselves to it with the same decisiveness and single-mindedness the merchant pursues his pearl.

If that's all there is to it, this parable is neither very original nor very interesting. The story is effective and the illustration is apt, but the point is rather obvious. Everybody already knows that the kingdom of God is the highest good, worth immea-surably more than anything we own. Everybody already knows that we should be ready to give everything to attain it. If this is what the parable means, then all it really does is find a clever way to make a point everybody already knows.

So we should wonder if that's all there is to it. If we recon-sider how the parable ends, we can pick up a hint that there may be more to it than the comfortable interpretation that so easily comes to mind. In fact, the end of the parable is not actually an ending at all, because the parable stops before the story it tells is over. The curtain falls with the merchant own-ing nothing except the pearl. Where can the merchant go from here? What does he do the day after? How does he make a living and support his family?

The apparent simplicity of the parable is deceptive. What at first sight seems like a happy ending is actually a no-win dilemma for the merchant. The beauty and value of the pearl so captivated him that he has left himself no means to continue his life. His situation is clearly untenable.

The genius of The Pearl is that it makes us finish the story. In the process of doing that, we can see that the parable is much more complex than it first appears. The parable seems to reinforce what we already know, but it leaves matters unfinished.

Of course, listeners can defeat the parable's challenge by taking its narrative as a complete story and its closing scene as a happy ending. However, those who read the parable this way are put in the same situation as the merchant: unwilling to accept the consequences of buying the pearl or, worse yet, unaware even that there are consequences. More perceptive listeners can resist the parable's challenge by objecting to its exaggerated terms, defending the merchant against the way the parable sets him up. No merchant with any sense would sell *everything* he owns. That is a reasonable objection, but it amounts to rejecting the parable as we have it in Matthew. (Those who object to the canonical version of The Pearl will prefer the one in the Gospel of Thomas. See the cameo essay.)

Of course no competent merchant would sell everything he owns. That's why I suggest that The Pearl portrays the merchant as a fool, in the sense that the term "fool" has in the Jewish wisdom tradition. In that tradition the essence of wisdom is living with the long-run in mind. The value of any course of action can be judged only retrospectively. Only from a course of action's "end" can its consequences be fully assessed. ("End," *acharit* in Hebrew, is a technical term in the wisdom tradition.) That is why the wisdom tradition places such a premium on the young learning from the elders, from those who have had enough experience to discern the likely outcomes of certain paths. The wise take the end into account and choose their paths accordingly. Those without wisdom are fools, that is, those who are attracted by what is immediate and act without knowledge or regard for long-term consequences. Two sayings from the Book of Proverbs can serve as classic illustrations of the importance of heeding the *acharit*. One saying warns against wine.

The Pearl in Thomas

The parable of the pearl occurs in the Gospel of Thomas as well as in Matthew.

> The Father's kingdom is like a merchant who had a supply of merchandise and then found a pearl. That merchant was prudent; he sold the merchandise and bought the single pearl for himself. (Thomas 76:1–2)

Although the two versions are quite similar, the few differences between them make a difference—a big one in fact. In Thomas the merchant is not a fool. On the contrary, he is "prudent." He avoids the fool's mistake of selling everything he owns; in Thomas the merchant sells "the merchandise" (his current inventory). After he buys the pearl Thomas' merchant still owns the necessities of life: his house, his furniture, his other belongings, and his shop. (If this parable were told today we'd have to add his car, computer, internet service, and cable television.) In Thomas the pearl is expensive but not even metaphorically priceless. A merchant comes across the opportunity to buy an expensive item at a high, but affordable, cost and responds prudently.

This version of The Pearl was lost until the discovery of the Gospel of Thomas in the mid-twentieth century. The only version known to Christians for about sixteen centuries was Matthew's and even today few are aware of Thomas' alternate version. It is therefore very interesting that the traditional interpretation of The Pearl—an interpretation in which the merchant responds appropriately and which fails to consider or probably even notice that he sells *everything* he owns and thus imperils his future—fits Thomas' version of the parable, not Matthew's. Ironic, no?

Do not look at wine when it is red,
when it sparkles in the cup and goes down smoothly.
In the *acharit* it bites like a serpent and stings like an
adder. (Prov 23:31–32)

Another saying warns unwary young men about the seduc-
tions of "strange" women.

The lips of a strange woman drip honey
and her speech is smoother than oil,
but in the *acharit* she is bitter as wormwood,
sharp as a two-edged sword. (Prov 5:3–4)

(It is unfortunate that major modern translations render *acharit*
in the above saying literally.)

In the wisdom tradition the fool is not a comic figure. The
fool is someone whose short-sightedness and immature judgment make him vulnerable to disasters that the wise know
how to avoid. Fools are a danger to themselves and to others,
not because they are malicious, but because they are foolish.

The Useless Treasure

The kingdom of heaven is like a treasure hidden in a
field. Someone found it, hid it, and out of joy goes and
sells everything he owns and buys that field. (Matt 13:44)

A treasure is like a "priceless" pearl, hugely valuable. But
while very few in Jesus' audience could picture themselves
buying a pearl, most of them could dream of finding treasure.
The land of Israel had been fought over many times over the
centuries. In wartime the only sure way to keep money from
being looted was to bury it. If the owner of that money was
killed, the secret of that treasure probably died with him. So
who knew how much was out there just waiting to be found?
It was a peasant's fantasy, the ancient analog to winning the
lottery: one stroke of unlikely luck that could catapult him
from debt to riches.

The parable of the treasure has the same narrative structure
as the parable of the pearl. A lucky discovery presents a man
with a once-in-a-lifetime opportunity, to which he responds

The Treasure of Immorality

The man who finds the treasure obtains it through fraud. If, as I argue below, the emergent context for the parable is Jesus' and his followers' reckless commitment to the kingdom of God, does the man's immoral behavior reflect something of that context? As I admitted earlier, we can do no more here than make guesses. Let me make two that go in opposite directions.

1. Perhaps the man's unethical tactics reflect Jesus' guilty conscience for sacrificing family bonds to the campaign for the kingdom of God. Several scenes and teachings in the gospels, which might be based on historical memories, clearly give the kingdom of God priority over family. Obligations to parents, spouses, children, and other relatives were considered sacred and walking away from them deemed gravely immoral. If the scene in which Jesus denies his mother and brothers (Mark 3:31–35) is based on some reality in the life of the historical Jesus, then he was in violation of the Fourth Commandment, "Honor your father and your mother." (*If* Jesus had a wife and children—this is doubtful but unknowable—and *if* he had walked away from them, his irresponsibility would be reprehensible.) The shame, pain, and deprivation caused by those who chose the kingdom over their families might explain why the parable tells of a man who cheated the landowner out of his treasure.

2. A more likely explanation of the man's unethical behavior in the parable has nothing to with its emergent context, but simply with the narrative logic of the story and Jesus' willingness to deploy immoral characters in his parables. The parable can end the way it does, that is, with a useless treasure, only if the man obtained it illegally. If he had acquired his treasure legally he would be free to spend it and the parable would have a "they all lived happily ever after" ending. So it is easy to account for the man's shady dealings without needing to imagine a corresponding real-life circumstance for Jesus and his followers. It is also the case that Jesus else-

where uses immoral characters without condemning their deeds: an embezzler (Luke 16:1–8), a murderous loan shark (Luke 19:11–27), and an assassin (Thomas 98). None of those characters should lead us to speculate about Jesus' own morals. Neither should the man in The Treasure.

with reckless determination, selling everything to obtain the fabulous object of his desire. As with The Pearl, The Treasure stops before it is over, leaving it to the audience to guess what happens next. At the end the treasure, like the pearl, is both immensely valuable and completely useless. In both parables the character turns out to be a fool facing a future emptied of assets. The two parables are, in effect, variations of the same story.

The parables differ only in two details. First, The Treasure is explicit about what motivated the man to buy the field: joy. That seemingly stray detail is actually crucial to my interpretation of the parable. (More on this later.) Second, the treasure finder acts immorally, obtaining the treasure through fraud. The treasure belongs to the original owner of the field, even if he doesn't know it is there. Since no legal process of "finders keepers" applied when it came to buried treasure, the man who finds it reburies it and buys the land. But he buys it without informing the seller of his discovery, thus defrauding the seller, who obviously would have taken the treasure for himself if he knew of its existence. No doubt the man who bought the field congratulates himself for pulling off this scam. But then what? If he spends a chunk of the treasure, people are going to wonder where he got the money. He sold everything he owned to buy the field, after which he owns it and nothing else. The village culture of Jesus and his audience allowed little or no privacy. Everyone knew everyone else's business. Everyone knew everyone's social and economic status. In a situation like that of Galilee at the time of Jesus, where most people live on the edge of subsistence, people are keenly aware of what might seem to us modest differences in economic status. No one can keep his wealth secret except by never spending it. If the man who bought the field starts to

live large, people will be suspicious; certainly the seller will cry
foul. And if the man lies and claims he found the treasure after
he bought the land, well, what would you think?

In the end (the *acharit*) the treasure turns out to be useless.
The man cannot spend it without exposing his own wrongdo-
ing. Having sold everything to buy the field, what now? His
situation is like the owner of the pearl, though in one way it
is better and one way it is worse. The man is in a worse situation than the merchant, who can, if he wishes, sell his pearl
and start over without legal complications. But the man with
the treasure cannot reverse what he has done without risk-
ing legal exposure (unless he reburies the treasure and walks
away from it—but what are the odds of that?). On the other
hand, while the merchant ends the story with nothing except
his pearl, the man with the useless treasure also has land, from
which he can make a living. He can't live like a rich man, but
at least he can live. But all this analysis assumes that the man
suddenly finds prudence and doesn't try to throw his new
money around. That seems an overly generous assumption for
someone imprudent enough to paint himself into a corner. In
any case it's beginning to feel as if we are pressing too hard on
minor differences between the two parables. Their similarities
are far more fundamental than their differences.

Context Matters

What are we to make of these strange stories? Each is well-
told, a finely-crafted miniature narrative. Each stops before
it ends, that is, before its story comes to a conclusion. That
effect flows so seamlessly from the narrative that it has to be
deliberate. If one of these parables had played out the story
to a conclusion that resolved the narrative suspense, we might
deduce that the abrupt non-ending of the other one was an
unfortunate result of inattentive storytelling. At least the complete story would give a strong clue as to how the incomplete
one should be finished. But since both parables stop before
their narratives are resolved, they must have been designed to
frustrate listeners and thus goad them to come up with their
own endings.

The Treasure in Thomas

Like The Pearl, The Treasure also occurs in an alternate version in the Gospel of Thomas.

> The kingdom is like a man who had a treasure hidden in his field but did not know about it. When he died he left it to his son. The son did not know about it either. He took over the field and sold it. The buyer went plowing, discovered the treasure, and began to lend money at interest to whomever he wished. (Thomas 109)

This story is quite different than the one in Matthew. Here the man who finds the treasure is not a fool. He does not sell everything to buy the field. For all we know, he does not have to sell anything. Unlike the case in Matthew, the treasure does not turn out to be useless; quite the contrary. Not only is the man free to spend the treasure, he makes money on it. Another important difference is that the man obtains the treasure honestly. And yet the treasure corrupts him. Lending money at interest to fellow Jews was forbidden by Torah. That he lends to Jews is clearly implied by "to whomever he wished."

★ ★ ★ ★ ★

Both The Pearl and The Treasure occur only in Matthew and Thomas. In Matthew both characters behave foolishly, but not in Thomas. Because the Matthean characters are fools, they end up facing untenable futures. For the Thomas characters, however, the future looks secure.

The foolish characters and their precarious futures are exactly the elements that make Matthew's versions of these stories so uncomfortable. Thus, when it comes to the two barbs in the stories, Matthew's versions of The Pearl and The Treasure have more in common with one another than either of them does with its counterpart in Thomas. Go figure.

One possible way forward is to posit an apocalyptic context within which these parables should be interpreted. If Jesus proclaimed an imminent apocalyptic kingdom of God, the non-endings to the parables make sense: selling all to gain the kingdom is a wise bargain. That the men in both parables are left with no real future is not a problem in an apocalyptic context because the imminence of the coming kingdom means there is no future for which one needs to provide. In this context the characters' recklessness demonstrates their discernment of how one should live in the End Times: without hedging bets and with a joyful confidence that all will be well without our having to arrange for it. In this apocalyptic reading of our two parables the men are positive models and Jesus is commending their behavior.

However, this interpretive path is a blind alley. That is because the decisions to sell everything are not motivated by an impending crisis. The apocalyptically appropriate behavior of selling all to gain the kingdom makes sense only if one does so *because* one believes the End is near. But the natural reading of the motives of the men in the parables goes in the opposite direction: they sell all to acquire the pearl/treasure and *then* find themselves without a future. It's not as if they realize that human history will soon be over and therefore sell all to acquire what is priceless.

In the Gospel of Mark—a gospel based on the conviction that the End was near (see Mark 9:1 and 13:29–30)—it is reasonable that if the rich young man wants "treasure in heaven" he should sell his possessions, give the money to the poor, and follow Jesus unreservedly (Mark 10:17–22). Note how Jesus' challenge to the rich man leaves no room for his obligations to those whose futures depend on him (his wife, children, or aged parents). In an apocalyptic context, like the one in which the Gospel of Mark was written, such obligations to the future are irrelevant. Outside that apocalyptic context (that is, if the world is not in its last days), it would be irresponsible and unethical for most people to do what Jesus recommends to the rich man. The only people who have the moral right to give away everything they own are those without social or family responsibilities.

Our two parables are not amenable to an apocalyptic interpretation and so our puzzle remains. They do not make much
sense by themselves. They clearly require *some* context. If not
apocalyptic, then what? For Jesus and the audiences to which
he pitched these parables, that context was their lived situation: what they brought to the telling and hearing of these oral
stories. The "meaning" in the parables would have emerged
in the give-and-take as people took Jesus' bait and finished
these stories in various ways, as they discussed and argued with
Jesus and among themselves over whether they approved of,
condemned, ridiculed, pitied, or sympathized with the characters in the stories. Unfortunately for us, those live exchanges,
charged as they must have been with various blends of enthu-
siasm, hostility, bafflement, curiosity, sarcasm, amusement, or
apathy are lost forever. All that we have left in the gospels is
the parables themselves—the conversation starters as it were. If
we take literally the teaching situations depicted in the gospels,
we are left with improbable or absurd scenarios of Jesus telling
parables that often take, as in this case, less than fifteen seconds,
to audiences who listen in silence. Then what?

Kinds of Contexts

The term "context" covers a lot of ground. It includes things
we know a great deal about, such as the religious, political,
historical, social, and linguistic frameworks within which Jesus
lived and taught (the realities often called "backgrounds").
But "context" also refers to the living contexts in which Jesus
spoke and people listened. Since those situational contexts
were specific to the time, place, and people addressed, they
would have been somewhat different each time Jesus retold a
parable. It is those situational contexts that are lost to us. When
they are supplied at all, the various elements of narrative setting in the gospels (the times, places, and audiences of specific
teachings) are the literary creations of the gospel writers. That
kind of information was not preserved in the oral tradition,
except in those few cases when an element of the narrative
setting is actually part of the teaching itself—for example, a

scene in which a healing provokes opposition because it is done on the Sabbath.

We need to make a distinction between two types of situational contexts: the context into which Jesus brought the parable and the context out of which the parable emerged. Asking about the latter, which I will call the "emergent context," means posing questions such as: what might have led Jesus to create this parable? or, to what is this parable a response? Obviously, there is little we can do to answer questions like those with much confidence. On rare occasions the literary settings of the parables in the gospels provide clues that make a lot of sense. For example, the mini-parable about the binding of the strong man (Mark 3:27) must have been a response to something pretty close to what the gospels depict: an accusation that Jesus was in cahoots with the devil (Mark 3:22). In the vast majority of cases, however, the gospel settings of the parables reflect only the creativity of the writers, and therefore most of the time we can only guess about the original contexts. So let me make a guess—an educated one, I hope—about the emergent context for The Pearl and The Treasure. Two considerations lead me to the speculation that follows. First, the context I propose is the only one I can think of that fits the peculiar contours of these frustratingly incomplete stories about fools; it is the only situation I can imagine to which these parables are apt (and weirdly wise) responses. Second, the context I propose has the ring of reality to it—it fits with other things we think are true about Jesus.

Jesus the Fool

I propose that The Treasure and The Pearl are autobiographical. Jesus tells these stories about himself, but not *only* about himself (see below). He sees himself in the merchant and the treasure seeker. In explaining my proposal I will focus on four elements in the parables. 1) The characters take single-minded and precipitous action (selling "everything"). 2) Their action leaves them with no discernible future. 3) The parables are about the kingdom of God. 4) The man who found the treasure acts the way he does out of joy.

1. The gospels portray Jesus as single-minded in his campaign on behalf of the kingdom of God. There is no mention of a wife or children. If Jesus once had a steady job, the gospels give the impression that he had left it. Of course, those silences in the gospels do not prove anything about the historical Jesus, but they do match the radical theme in his teaching about holding nothing back from the service of God. If Jesus believed everything he taught and if he truly tried to live by all of it—and these are two big and unprovable ifs—then the gospel portrait of him as a man driven by his passion for his mission is what you might expect from someone who taught what he did.

2. Jesus campaigned for the kingdom of God as if there was no tomorrow. By this I don't mean that Jesus was an apocalyptic prophet announcing that the End was near. What I mean is that he challenged others not to worry about the future and to trust God to supply the needs of the day (see, for example, Luke 12:22–31). My hunch is that he tried to live that way himself. But living that way is irresponsible for someone with family obligations. Even if Jesus had no wife or children, he had at least a mother to whom he had responsibilities. Mark's gospel just might preserve an historical memory of Jesus' ruptured relationship with his family of origin: they come to take him away because he's acting crazy (Mark 3:21) and he in turn disowns them (3:31–35). The shock in this scene gives it the ring of authenticity. Jesus' "crazy" behavior worried those who loved him and brought shame on his family. Both are plausible motives for their attempt to "seize" him (as Mark puts it) and take him back home, thereby shutting down his campaign. (No wonder that this verse [Mark 3:21] is one of only a handful in Mark that both Matthew and Luke independently deleted—apparently neither could find a way to salvage it through rewriting.) Jesus' response, in effect disowning his family, is the ultimate act of disrespect. No greater insult is possible in ancient Jewish culture. If this scene is based on authentic memories—and it just might be: the Jesus Seminar colored this passage pink—Jesus' behavior would have discredited him in the eyes of just about everyone who knew about it. Luke does not delete this scene, but he does sanitize

it (Luke 8:19–21), reversing Mark's meaning by rewriting the scene to ensure that Jesus *includes* his mother and brothers in his enlarged family.

Without a family Jesus' own future was precarious, for family was the only social safety net in the ancient world. But this in itself would not necessarily put his future at risk. What did that was his public proclamation of the kingdom of God.

3. The term "kingdom" (*basileia* in Greek) was an overtly political term. Herod was a king (*basileus*) who ruled Galilee at the pleasure of the Romans. Pilate ruled Judea as part of the *basileia* of Rome. The Latin word for *basileia* is *imperium*, the source of our word "empire." To assert that any other kingdom/empire had a claim on people was to challenge the authority of Rome, which enforced its *basileia* through the threat of overwhelming and appalling violence. When Jesus challenged people to live in the *basileia* of God he was defying Roman authority. That symbolic meaning was as obvious then as burning the American flag is now. It didn't need any explaining. And proclaiming God's *basileia* was far more dangerous than burning a flag is today. Jesus realized the danger, of course. He had seen what had happened to his mentor, John, when the Baptizer had antagonized the *basileus*. Galilee was a small place and Herod was doubtlessly monitoring potential threats to his power through a network of informants. When Jesus spoke of the kingdom of God to strangers, the thought must often have crossed his mind that in his audience there might be those willing to inform on him.

Jesus didn't need supernatural powers to foresee that a continued public campaign for the kingdom of God could well end very badly for him. He would have had to be incredibly naïve to think otherwise. Perhaps part of him hoped that God would keep him safe. After all, Jesus knew the stories of how Joseph was rescued from the well, Jeremiah from the cistern, Daniel from the lions, and Susanna from the lies of wicked men. But Jesus also knew that God had not rescued his prophet John. Having lived his whole life in Rome's *basileia*, Jesus had surely seen crucified men. He surely understood the unmistakable lesson Rome was teaching through the broken bodies and crushed spirits of those victims of Roman law-and-order. I therefore think it highly likely that Jesus continued with his campaign in the awareness that it might lead him to a Roman cross.

In the Face of Danger

Why did Jesus continue on such a dangerous path? The traditional answer, as old as Christianity itself, and spelled out explicitly from the earliest gospel, is that Jesus' death *was* his mission. (Ask ten Christians on the street why Jesus came to earth and probably eight or nine will say, "to die for our sins.") For traditional Christianity there is no mystery why Jesus chose a path that put his life at risk: he did that *in order to* die on a cross and in the knowledge that he would be resurrected within thirty-six hours. Of course, that answer presupposes that Jesus had supernatural knowledge of the future and knew himself to be the divine Son of God. But since such presuppositions are in principle unverifiable historically, they cannot be used in our attempts to understand the historical Jesus. (The traditional answer also entails the ugly image of a god who demands the blood of the innocent in order to forgive sin—but that is another story.)

Martyrs may seek death for various reasons: as a ticket to immortality, as a dramatic end to redeem a compromised life, or as suicide at the hands of others.[1] But other martyrs (most of them, I hope) do not want to be killed. They seek justice or integrity or truth, and they accept violent death as its price. Imagine a martyr awaiting execution. What happens if mercy unexpectedly prevails and the would-be martyr is set free? The first kind of martyr would be frustrated, the second kind

---

1. Suicide bombers are not martyrs, despite the way some Muslims regard them. By my definition a martyr is one who accepts death as a witness to the rightness of his or her cause, but is unwilling to kill others. Those who kill themselves while trying to kill others are not martyrs. If their targets are military, they are suicide warriors like the kamikaze pilots. If they target civilians, they are murderers.

relieved (to put it mildly). The second kind might blurt out a spontaneous prayer of thanks; what spontaneous emotion would the first kind have to repress?

The historical Jesus was not a death-seeking martyr. Nothing in his teaching says or implies that the cause of God's kingdom is advanced by the violent death of the innocent, or of the guilty for that matter. On the contrary, the vision of God's kingdom refracted through the teachings and deeds of the historical Jesus associates it with cherishing and sharing God's gift of life. It also calls on people to resist whatever impedes that cherishing through such practices as sharing food, healing the sick, establishing justice for the poor, canceling debts, and forgiving those who don't deserve it.[2] Jesus accepted the prospect of his own violent death as a possible, or even likely, outcome of his campaign on behalf of God's kingdom, but Jesus did not seek his own death. He campaigned for the kingdom despite, not because of, the death to which it might lead him.

4. Now back to the question of what impelled Jesus to continue in the face of such appalling danger. I believe the answer is explicit in The Treasure and implicit in The Pearl: joy. (Although joy is not mentioned in The Pearl, it is so appropriate there that it is difficult not to include it in our thoughts about that story.) Both the treasure seeker and, I assume, the merchant make rash and unconditional decisions *out of joy*; both are blinded by the promise of what they see before them. Without counting the cost they throw away their futures out of joy at their discoveries. At the non-end of each of their stories, many in the audience will think them foolish (that is, not aware of what's truly good for them) and naïve (not taking

---

2. Many readers know this already, but it cannot be repeated too often: for the historical Jesus, the kingdom of God was an earthly reality, not something up in heaven after death. (The expression "kingdom of heaven" in Matthew's gospel is a Jewish circumlocution for "kingdom of God"; the kingdom *of* heaven is not *in* heaven.) For Jesus "kingdom of God" referred to the way the world works when it runs according to God's will, rather than according to Rome's will. It is, if you will, "heaven on earth."

into account the way the real world works). But the characters surely consider themselves lucky beyond their dreams, as if their whole lives had been building up to that moment. The artfulness of these parables shows through in the spontaneity with which both characters seize their opportunities and leap before looking. It is as if they could not do otherwise.

I imagine that Jesus told these parables when anxious followers and those who cared about him asked where he thought his path would lead. "What good can come from all this? Do you think the authorities will let you get away with this? Look what they did to John!" Jesus tells these parables because he has no answer to those perfectly rational questions. He cannot refute the objection that his behavior is naïve, and he cannot gainsay the criticism that his campaign might well end very, very badly. But what else can he do? His vision of the kingdom of God and his experience of it in the healing of the sick, the sharing with the hungry, the acceptance of the outcast, etc. is a priceless pearl and a treasure beyond counting. To communicate his vision of that kingdom in his teaching, to spread it through his deeds, and to coax, encourage, and enable others to dare to live in that kingdom—that is what he was meant to do. That is his God-given mission. His whole life has been leading up to it. He cannot do otherwise.

Our two parables are about Jesus, but not about him alone. They apply equally to those who were captivated by his vision and threw in their lot with his. Their futures are as opaque and insecure as his. After Jesus' death some early Christians, and a very few modern ones too, could with equal justification retell these parables about themselves.

And yet to say that these parables are *about* Jesus and his followers is to speak loosely. To put it more precisely, and using the terminology I introduced earlier, the predicament of Jesus and his followers is the emergent context of these parables. Their predicament illuminates the circumstances that called forth these parables from Jesus' poetic imagination. But what the parables are properly *about* is exactly what they say they are about: the kingdom of God. It is because the kingdom of God is what it is that Jesus and his crew find themselves where they are, blinded by its beauty and goodness. It is because of that kingdom that they are unwilling to envision a future for themselves in which they are not committed to it. They cannot do otherwise.

Chapter Eight

Jesus after Hamlet

A Path from Elsinore to Nazareth?

Edward F. Beutner

"Things throw light on things,
And all the stones have wings."
—Theodore Roethke

Harold Bloom once tossed out a tempting morsel, an isolated sentence in which he spoke of both Shakespeare's
Hamlet and Mark's Jesus as characters who come to us as literary re-inventions of the human (Bloom, 1998).

Having gnawed a bit on Bloom's discarded tidbit, I want to
argue for a link between these two unlikely and very disparate
tragic heroes, Jesus and Hamlet. This exploration of Harold
Bloom's suggestion addresses and clarifies the following questions as well: Why do tragic heroes exist at all; why do we first
anoint and then elevate them; and why do we celebrate them
endlessly?

Despite the world of differences between them, Hamlet and
Jesus share an imaginative faculty: while remaining inhabitants
of their own peculiar times and stations, their depth of vision

The Fourth R 16,1 (2003), 9–14

and fecundity of expression have exercised so firm and durable a hold on human consciousness that from their own day to the present they have both been understood as our permanent contemporaries. Both Jesus and Hamlet are tragic heroes whose power to transform their listeners derives not from any staginess in their few external exploits, but from the profound generativity of their every abundant utterance.

The image of the tragic hero looms large in the communal imagination when set side by side with the humdrum and anonymous everydayness of our ordinary lives. As Americans, we are incessantly bombarded by the myth that the only hero worthy of our worship is the tough good-guy, the reluctant bully who will blaze or blast a path toward dominance of others and control of external events. We need to be disabused of that pervasive myth and reminded that our need for heroes is not in every case a need for action figures. Sometimes we yearn more simply and deeply for models who will provide and enhance meaning within the human predicament, quite aside from the question of whether or not the course of history has been altered by their personal exploits.

In some cases a tragic hero's voice will far surpass his deeds. Think Prometheus, Gandhi, Lear; think Hamlet, Job or Jesus. Say what you will about their control of events, their voices have endured. The words they speak are percussive as thunder and incisive as lightning. They cut us to the quick. We celebrate these protagonists because they come to meet us neither as conquering heroes nor as hapless ciphers, but each as a distinctive brilliant star demarking an otherwise massive, blurry human universe.

Northrop Frye observes that tragic heroes appear head and shoulders above the rest of us (we constitute both their context and their audience) not only because of our yearning to live at their exalted level, but also because there is "something unnamed, something on the other side of tragic heroes, opposite the audience, compared to which even the heroes themselves are small" (Frye, 1957). This "something else" we have no descriptive word for; accordingly we rummage through our lexicons for multiple terms: God, the gods, fate, accident, fortune, destiny, necessity, circumstance, providence—or any combination of these descriptors. But whatever that "something other" may be called, Frye identifies the tragic hero as mediator between us and that otherness.

Tragic heroes are those we locate atop a mountain, a dunghill, a castle, or a scaffold—midway between human society on the ground and the something greater that may be lurking silently backstage or hiding invisibly in the sky. They are suspended between a world of unfettered freedom and a world of debasing bondage. Frye specifies their function:

> Tragic heroes are so much the highest points in their human landscape that they seem the inevitable conductors of the power about them; great trees more likely to be struck by lightning than a clump of grass. . . . Tragic heroes are wrapped in the mystery of their communion with that something beyond which we can see only through them, and which is the source of their strength and of their fate alike. (Frye, 1957)

I repeat with utmost emphasis that Hamlet is not Jesus, nor Jesus Hamlet. There needs no ghost come from the grave to tell us this. The Dane is an introverted loner who'd like to set things right (o cursed spite!); the Nazarene is more a bantering socializer who embraces the good and bad alike. Their temperaments could hardly be more different. That said, there remains a point of comparison well worth introducing: each is a tragic hero from the distant past who remains widely celebrated—a status that in our time has often meant elevation to the movie screen.

First a further word about what I have proposed these two heroes have in common, then on to a recommendation of a particular *Hamlet*, the recent film which spells out in the character of Hamlet certain uncommon qualities that might well spill over into our appreciation of Jesus—that is, should anyone be willing to assume the burden of portraying Jesus, like Hamlet, as a figure whose speech is at least as compelling as the events he is caught up in but cannot control.

Among Prince Hamlet's definitional problems, the chief one is typically Elizabethan, and accordingly belongs to the audience of Hamlet as well: how to behave as prince—how to fulfill one's role and occupy one's place in a system which defined a person according to a strictly pre-assigned position within the larger feudal system (Howard, 1970). In a word, how to know one's place, and then to keep it.

Now add to this Hamlet's gifted sensibility, his acute awareness of the tragic consequences of behaving in blind, unquestioning accordance with his role as prince and heir apparent. He is pulled, like all of us, in two directions at once. Either pure compliance or bold defiance will upset his inner gyroscope because both involve self-compromise. So Hamlet's life becomes a tightrope walk, and to confront it with accord, integrity, and grit, he must delve deep inside himself to find a world he much admires, but has not quite yet tried on for size.

This future for which Hamlet yearns is a world that affirms and celebrates the variety and capacity of the individual human being as something more than mere pawn or functionary. Even in his more despairing and self-exasperated moments, and maybe even especially then, Hamlet abruptly changes his tune and gives voice to his inner vision in words often quoted and more than once described as the highly intuitive voice of the Renaissance:

> What a piece of work is man! How noble in reason!
> How infinite in faculty! In form and moving how express
> and admirable! In action how like an angel! In apprehen-
> sion how like a god! The beauty of the world! The para-
> gon of animals! (*Hamlet*, Act II, Scene ii, 293–297)

The issue Hamlet faces is more than merely intellectual. He experiences Denmark, a world of fixed stability, as every inch a prison. He knows that even if or when such a sedimented or received world (Funk's terms, 1966) were governed honestly, it would remain structurally too constrictive, and far too rigid and asphixiant for the "form and moving of so express and admirable a piece of work as man." The conflict Hamlet expresses and embodies for his audience is that of the elevated tragic hero torn between the unquestioned dictates of fixed traditions and his own convincing vision of the inviolable trustworthiness of individual human freedom, genius, conscience.

Jesus, like Hamlet, is presented as a man caught between two opposing worlds. No less than the rest of us, both Hamlet and Jesus are betrayed in their revealing and transparent utterances. I do not mean by this that Hamlet, Jesus, or any of the rest of us can resolve life's dilemmas with words alone, or with clever phrases. Hamlet makes this clear over and over again in the play: words will not suffice! Belief in the efficacy of words alone, in fact, represents the kind of default world (Scott's term, 2002) that ends up defending such notions as verbal inspiration, or crediting the recitation of magic formulas for the banishment of evil—the kind of pseudo-religion which Karl Rahner dismisses with a single disdainful word of his own: ortholalia (reciting magic formulas).

What I mean to say about the speech of Hamlet and Jesus in relation to the rest of us is this: all former and familiar ways of seeing things are bound to produce no more than fixed and shopworn discourse, however cleverly reshuffled or recycled. Untested and exotic visions and convictions, on the other hand, will inevitably find tongue in strange and unfamiliar expressions of epiphany. Both Jesus and Hamlet were thought mad, even by their intimates (Mark 3:21; *Hamlet*, Act II, Scene 2, passim), yet each invites his listeners to grasp the method in his madness. The method of metaphor delivers their listeners from the madness of myth.

New language traditions are born, after all, not *in order* to usher in a world of meaning once thought to be unthinkable, but *as a result of* that new worldview that they both proceed from and proclaim. Under the pressure of the new and heady vision, the old accepted rhetoric, along with the effete world that it sanctions and supports, eventually breaks apart at the seams. The experimental language becomes, so to speak, the not-quite-unfurled flag of a newborn world coming barely into being.

Since brevity is the soul of wit, I will be brief: in the play *Hamlet*, Polonius is the proponent of the old rhetoric, tried and true; whereas Hamlet ushers in the utterly new. In the New Testament, Jesus acts and utters that which is new, whereas John the Baptist is proponent of the old.

I would argue, then, that this creative consciousness is what our two tragic heroes have significantly in common, and that it is, in both cases, the quality most worth noticing in each of them. Accordingly, I would suggest the need for a play or movie that presents Jesus as a tragic hero, but with less emphasis on the ordeals he undergoes, and with a more compelling portrayal of how he evaluates and expresses, like Hamlet after him, all that is going on around him, about him, and most of all within him.

To readers who doubt that such a portrayal of Jesus (that is, with his brilliant banter brought front and center) would make for compelling drama, I can only recommend the recent *Hamlet* played and directed by Campbell Scott, and then gladly leave to their imagination both the inner affinities between Jesus and Hamlet and the as-yet untested cinematic possibilities inherent in the interplay.

In loving memory of Bill Stock, a fellow of desiccate jest.

Chapter Nine

Jesus of Nazareth

A Glimpse

Robert W. Funk

Voice Print

The theme of Jesus' public discourse was the kingdom of God or God's domain. God's domain was that region or sphere where God's dominion was immediate and absolute. Jesus believed God's reign to be present, but not discernible to ordinary eyes.

Jesus' characteristic speech forms include parables and aphorisms.

A parable is a short, short story that confronts the hearer with a dilemma and then invites that hearer to make a choice. The laborers in the vineyard, the great supper, the prodigal, the Samaritan, the dishonest manager, and the unforgiving slave are parables.

An aphorism is a proverb that subverts conventional wisdom. Aphorisms never articulate the whole truth; they express either a half-truth or a truth-and-a-half. "An apple a day keeps the doctor away" is a proverb. "It is easier for a camel to squeeze through the eye of a needle than for someone with wealth to enter God's domain" is an aphorism. Acts of char-

The Fourth R 9,1/2 (1996) 17–20

ity were enjoined proverbially in Israel; Jesus takes the proverb one step further and turns it into an aphorism: "Give to everyone who begs from you." That is a parody of conventional values. "Love your enemies" is a paradox. He also coined short, witty hyperboles such as: "You see the sliver in your friend's eye, but don't notice the timber sticking out of your own."

Jesus always talked about God's reign in everyday, mundane terms—dinner parties, travelers being mugged, truant sons, laborers in a vineyard, the hungry and tearful. His language was concrete and specific. He did not cite and interpret scripture. He never used abstract language. He made no theological statements. He would not have said, "I believe in God the Father Almighty." Or "all human beings have sinned and fallen short of the glory of God." Or "I think, therefore I am." It never occurred to him to assert that God is love. Jesus did not have a doctrine of God; he had only experience of God.

Although his language was drawn from the mundane world about him, he did not have ordinary reality in mind when he spoke about God's estate. His language is indirect; it is highly figurative, metaphorical, or non-literal. The parable of the leaven is not about baking bread. The mustard seed and sower are not about gardening. The Samaritan is not about a robbery on the Jericho road. His admonition to lend to everyone who wants to borrow has no reference to banking practice.

Jesus' forms of speech were laced with tension. Forms of tension include conjoining the literal to the figurative; the use of exaggeration, caricature, paradox, and parody; the articulation of global injunctions that are impossible of execution. His parables and aphorisms regularly frustrate the expectations of his hearers.

Jesus was plied with questions, to which he never gave a direct answer. "Should we pay taxes," he was asked. "Pay the emperor what is due the emperor and pay God what is due God" was his ambiguous response.

Jesus may be described as a comic savant. He was perhaps the first standup Jewish comic. A comic savant is a sage who embeds wisdom in humor; a humorist shuns practical advice. Comic wisdom refuses to be explicit. Yet in the stories he tells, the sage constructs a new fiction that becomes the basis for his or her own action and the action of others. The contours of that fiction are ambiguous in order to frustrate moralizing proclivities, and are polyvalent as a way to keep them open to reinterpretation in new contexts.

Visionary Sage

Jesus was an iconoclastic Jewish poet who spoke three languages: Aramaic, Greek, and parable. His parables and witticisms are a knothole in the cosmic fence that fronts the alternative reality he called the kingdom of God. Through that aperture we get a glimpse of the world as Jesus saw it.

Jesus told his parables as though he were hearing them. Rather than making a claim for himself or for his Father, he was allowing himself to be claimed by his vision.

Jesus celebrated life as though he had just discovered a cache of coins, been invited to a state banquet, been royally received as a long lost son or daughter.

As a Jewish comic, he caricatured human behavior by exaggerating human foibles, poking fun at pomposity, especially on the part of religious authorities, and lampooning the public demonstration of piety. He advised his followers to pray out of earshot of everyone but God; where acts of charity were concerned, he suggested that the left hand should be kept in the dark about what the right hand was up to.

Jesus practiced and advocated an unbrokered relationship to God: for him temple and priests were redundant.

Trust in the God who inventories the hairs on human heads should rob humans of any anxiety about food, drink, and clothing. Perhaps that is the reason he advised his followers, no doubt in jest, to surrender both garments and go naked when sued for their coat as security for a debt.

The great barrier blocking the entrance to the kingdom was reliance on wealth: camels pass through the eye of needles more readily than do humans trying to squeeze through the kingdom's gate with their worldly possessions in tow.

Jesus advocated replacing blood relationships with true relatives: "Unless you hate your father and mother, wife and children, brothers and sisters, you're no disciple of mine," he said. True relatives are those who do the will of God.

Jesus took the right of forgiveness out of the hands of God and priest and reassigned it exclusively to those who needed it: to be forgiven, all one need do is forgive.

In the body of authentic lore that originated with Jesus, he asked not one thing for himself and taught his followers to ask only for bread for the day—nothing more.

Jesus denied his followers any sense of or right to Christian "privilege." One can be first only by being last. One can preserve life only by losing it. Like the prodigal, one can come home only by perpetually leaving home.

Jesus was not merely a victim; he was the victim of his own vision. The cross for Jesus and the hemlock for Socrates are symbols of uncompromising integrity.

Very early on the followers of Jesus exchanged the vision for the visionary; they turned the iconoclast into an icon. They domesticated his teachings and marketed him as the expected messiah. They had visions of him risen from the dead. They believed he had been sent from God.

What Jesus Wasn't and the Kingdom Isn't

The distinction between the gospel of Jesus and the Jesus of the gospels permits one to summarize what Jesus wasn't and the kingdom isn't. It is as important to specify what Jesus was not as it is to indicate what he really said and did. In this we are only following the practice of Jesus in frustrating inherited expectations.

1. Jesus did not think a cosmic holocaust would take place in his own time, unlike John the Baptist and many others. He thought God's kingdom was arriving unnoticed.
2. Jesus did not ask his followers to believe that he was the messiah. He certainly never suggested that he was the second person of the trinity. He rarely referred to himself

at all, and when he did, he thought of himself only as homeless.

3. Unlike his mentor, John the Baptist, Jesus did not call on people to repent, or fast, or observe the Sabbath. He did not threaten with hell or promise heaven.

4. Jesus did not ask his followers to believe that he was conceived without male sperm or that his mother was a virgin.

5. Jesus did not ask his followers to believe that he would be raised from the dead.

6. Jesus did not suggest that his death would be a blood sacrifice, that he was going to die for the sins of humankind.

7. Jesus did not regard scripture as infallible or even inspired; he taught on the basis of a new authority, the authority inherent in his words and deeds.

8. Jesus did not organize a church, appoint clergy, or advocate celibacy.

9. Jesus did not predict that he would return someday as the son of Adam and sit in judgment on the world.

Chapter Ten

The Reappearance of Parables

Bernard Brandon Scott

How should I go about putting together a profile of
Jesus? I could construct a "life" of Jesus. There is much
to speak for such a suggestion because a story of Jesus' life
would make it easier to make sense of it, to see how it fits
together. However, one of the assured results of 150 years of
the quest for the historical Jesus is that we do not have enough
evidence to know how to construct such an outline. The only
outline we have is the one created by the author of the Gospel
according to Mark.

I have chosen a different path. I have taken the material,
both sayings and deeds, that has the highest claim to be from
Jesus and have asked how this material coheres. How does it fit
together? Does it represent a consistent picture? After develop-
ing three theses which I think represent this coherent view of
Jesus' sayings and deeds, I then will ask what this tells us about
the personality of Jesus.

The Fourth R 10,1/2 (1997), 3–14

The Disappearance of Parables

There is general consensus among scholars that the quest of the historical Jesus has entered a new stage since the mid-1980's. A characteristic of recent books about the historical Jesus—a trend that cuts across all of them—is the disappearance of parables. At one level this is understandable because recent scholars have sought to shift the quest from the sayings of Jesus to the deeds. The previous generation of scholars had stressed the sayings and teachings of Jesus. This made the disappearance of parables inevitable.

The motives of individual authors vary. E. P. Sanders in his *Jesus and Judaism* distrusts language because it needs interpretation and there is no way to secure that interpretation. So he turned his attention to deeds that provided the sure foundation. John P. Meier in volume two of his *A Marginal Jew* dismisses parable interpretation because he neither approves of the methodology nor the current direction of parable studies. He attempts to figure out what the parables mean by predefining what the kingdom of God means. The kingdom of God determines the meaning of the parable rather than the parable defining the kingdom of God. Because of this procedure, one can for all practical purposes dismiss the parables.

John Dominic Crossan, who had established his early reputation as parable scholar, makes minimal use of parables in his *The Historical Jesus*. Since he selects only material that is from the earliest stages of the Jesus tradition and that occurs in multiple independent witnesses, few parables get through his sieve.

Finally, Marcus Borg in his *Meeting Jesus Again for the First Time* employs the insights from the parable studies of Robert Funk and Crossan in seeing the world turned upside down, but parables themselves are peripheral to his understanding of Jesus as a charismatic figure.

The Reappearance of Parables

I have chosen to base my profile on the parables for two reasons. (1) Proverbs, aphoristic sayings and parables dominate the database of Jesus sayings, and (2) the parables of Jesus are a distinctive literary form within that group of sayings. Despite various assertions to the contrary, there is no evidence of parable tellers contemporary with Jesus. The rabbinic parable develops after the destruction of the temple in 70 CE and follows a very different stereotyped use. Even more, many forms in the Jesus database that are not parables often have a "parabolic" twist. For example, the Other Cheek or Coat and Shirt turn out to be burlesques of codified law, rather than the exact codification of case law. If when someone asked for my shirt I also gave him my coat, I would soon be naked. That is, these exhibit what I and others have called the distinctive voice of Jesus.

In what follows I have developed three different nodes of relative historical certainty. Each one is represented by a parable that provides the insight that allows me to sketch the general contour of the node. I will expand the insight by relating various other sayings and deeds to form a coherent picture of each node. I have not engaged in a detailed analysis of each saying, but rely upon the work done in my *Hear Then the Parable*.

NODE ONE The Leaven

In the voting of the Jesus Seminar, the parable of the Leaven attracted the highest ranking of any parable. The Fellows considered it the most likely of all Jesus' parables to be authentic. I take that to be significant for two reasons. It has not figured strongly in anybody's reconstruction of the historical Jesus and receives little attention in the history of scholarship. Also it indicates that the radical interpretation of this parable initiated by Funk in *Jesus as Precursor* has won the day. Here if anywhere the distinctive voice of Jesus can be heard.

INSIGHT God becomes unclean

The parable serves as vehicle for the "kingdom of God." How to translate the phrase "kingdom of God" has provoked much discussion. Some prefer "the ruling activity of God," while others have suggested "imperial rule of God," and still oth-

Node One

Able-bodied and sick
POxy 1224 5:2,★ Matt 9:12, Mark 2:17,
Luke 5:31

Assassin
Thom 98:1-3

Congratulations: hungry
Luke 6:21, Matt 5:6, Thom 69:2

Congratulations: poor
Luke 6:20, Thom 54, Matt 5:3

Congratulations: sad
Luke 6:21, Matt 5:4

Corrupt judge
Luke 18:2-5

Eye of a needle
Matt 19:24, Luke 18:25, Mark 10:25

Foxes have dens
Luke 9:58, Matt 8:20, Thom 86:1-2

Leaven
Luke 13:20-21, Matt 13:33, Thom 96:1-2

Mustard seed
Thom 20:2-4, Mark 4:30-32, Luke 13:18-
19, Matt 13:31-32

No respect at home
Thom 31:1, Luke 4:24, John 4:44, Matt
13:57, Mark 6:4

Scholars' privileges
Luke 20:46, Mark 12:38-39, Matt 23:5-7,
Luke 11:43

Shrewd manager
Luke 16:1-8

Sly as a snake
Matt 10:16, Thom 39:3

Toll collector and Pharisee
Luke 18:10-14

Treasure
Matt 13:44, Thom 109:1-3

Two friends at midnight
Luke 11:5-8

What goes in
Mark 7:14-15, Thom 14:5, Matt 15:10-11

The texts that provide the
database for the first node of
relative historical certainty,
leading to the insight that in
Jesus' parables and aphorisms,
God becomes unclean.

★The texts of Papyrus
Oxyrhynchus 1224 and
the Gospel of Thomas can
be found in *The Complete
Gospels*.

ers "God's domain." The problem with "kingdom" is that the word in English is too vague, too ethereal. The more exact term is "empire" because the dominant political reality of the ancient world was the empire. So I prefer to translate this phrase "the Empire of God." Empire suggests a stronger, more dominant reality and has the virtue of implying its opposite. The opposite of the Empire of God is the Roman Empire. If the term has negative overtones in English, that is all right, because empires had bad reputations in the ancient world.

The parable of the Leaven arranges a series of words into a pattern that the hearer must decode. We can view the parable at two different levels.

At the level of a sentence the parable appears to picture an everyday scene in which a woman mixes some leaven in dough to make bread. But even at the sentence level there are some oddities. The woman hides the leaven. She does not mix the leaven, as one might expect. Likewise, the Greek word used here is not the neutral Greek word for hiding, but a word with strong negative overtones. She conceals the leaven in the dough. Even more, the amount of dough is extraordinary. Three measures is about forty pounds of flour, not the normal amount for a baking session. It produces a humorous image of the woman baking such a large amount, surely for a party. So while at the level of a simple sentence the parable appears to be everyday, upon closer examination there are suggestions that things are not quite normal.

The second level at which to understand the parable is as a metaphor or comparison for the Empire of God. At this level it produces a cacophony. Leaven is a symbol for moral evil, the unclean; unleaven is the proper symbol for the divine. According to Exodus, at Passover "For seven days no leaven shall be found in your houses; for if any one eats what is leavened, that person shall be cut off from the congregation of Israel" (12:19). Twice Paul quotes the proverb "A little leaven leavens the whole lump" to warn that a little evil will corrupt everything (Gal 5:9; 1 Cor 5:7). It parallels the American aphorism "One rotten apple spoils the whole barrel." And Jesus warns his disciples to "beware of the leaven of the Pharisees"

(Mark 8:15). It is not too extreme to say that the juxtaposition of Empire of God and leaven is blasphemous. The comparison of the Empire of Rome to leaven would be more appropriate.

Besides this initial negative symbol, the parable piles on other problematic symbols: a woman hides or conceals until all is leavened. Woman represents female shame as opposed to male honor. "Until it is all leavened" brings the process of corruption to completion. The only symbolically positive term in the parable is "three measures," which is probably a reference to the messianic banquet. When Abraham receives the three angelic messengers at the Oaks of Mamre, Sarah makes cakes from three measures of flour (Gen 18:6). The reference in the parable to three measures is where the parable at the sentence level bursts out of the everyday, because the amount is way beyond ordinary. It points to the extraordinary, a divine banquet.

This one-sentence parable redefines the divine. The divine is identified with the unclean, the impure. The involvement of the divine with the unclean does not result in the unclean becoming clean. The parable does not end with "until it was all unleavened." Rather the divine becomes unclean—or to restate this insight even more provocatively, God becomes unclean. This is the fundamental insight on which I will build a profile of Jesus.

CONVERGENCE Snakes and doves

In this section I want to show how this initial insight converges with other items from the database. This allows further expansion of the insight as well as producing what I hope is a convincing pattern within the database. This pattern or arrangement should begin to make sense of the isolated sayings and deeds.

The insight that God becomes unclean goes a long way toward explaining the frequent references to Jesus' association with outcasts, lepers, and sinners and the special place of women in his activity. These people find themselves accepted as they are, without the need to become clean or honorable. The Congratulations also belong to this node, for they con-

gratulate people who are not obviously to be congratulated.
The poor are congratulated because they are poor and to them
belongs the Empire of God, not because they will be rich.
This overturns the assumption that poverty and disease are
God's punishment for sins that underlies biblical books from
Deuteronomy to 2 Kings.

The saying What Goes In explicitly applies this insight to
food laws. This argument—that it is not what goes into the
mouth that defiles a person, but what comes out—upsets the
ability of the food laws to define what is clean and holy. Jesus
appears to have carried out this aphorism literally in his eating
habits by not washing his hands and by eating with "unclean"
people—toll collectors, lepers, and so on. The function of food
laws is to codify the divine so one can know where the divine
is. But if foods can no longer represent and replicate the divine
by marking the line between clean and unclean, then people
can no longer be divided into clean and unclean.

This same rejection of the line between the clean and
unclean finds expression in several parables. In the Mustard
Seed the planting of mustard seed, a weed-like plant, pollutes
the garden, makes it unclean. Various revisions of the parable
have obscured this aspect, though it is clearly present in the
Lukan version. Likewise, Crossan has shown in his analysis of
the parable of the Treasure that the treasure, a gift, becomes a
seduction for the man who, in his joy at finding the treasure,
rushes out to do an immoral thing. He buries the treasure in
a field and then goes and buys the field, thus signaling that
the treasure is not his. He steals it from its rightful owner. This
parable is a counterpoint to the Leaven. What is good, a treasure, seduces the man into doing evil.

Belonging to this same node is the Eye of a Needle. The
rich man is like treasure. He should be congratulated according to Deuteronomy, but it will be more difficult for him to
enter the Empire of God than for a camel to pass through the
eye of needle.

Likewise the warning against the Privileges of Scholars,
"who like to parade around in long robes" belongs here.
Scholars know what is clean and unclean and can thus represent the divine. But they should not be imitated, for the basis

on which their scholarship rests has been undermined. The complex of sayings dealing with the Able-bodied and Sick clearly indicate that God is on the side of the sick. It is they who need a physician. God identifies not with the honorable and righteous, but with the shamed and sinners.

Finally, into this node I would place those parables that exhibit characters that do not quite seem to conform to the standard of behavior thought appropriate to the Empire of God. For example, the violence of the Assassin who tests his power by thrusting his sword through a wall shocks a hearer. Like the man who finds Treasure, the wheeling and dealing of the Shrewd Manager has confounded various interpreters since before the parable was incorporated into the gospel tradition. When dismissed from his job as steward, he goes to those who owe a debt to his master and drastically reduces their debt.

The shamelessness of the man who delays in welcoming his guest in Two Friends at Midnight and the Corrupt Judge who fears neither God nor people in dealing with the widow's request both exhibit behavior that confounds an audience. The very amorality of the parables has proven problematic for most interpreters, to the point that the tradition has tried to explain it away. In the end, it is the Toll Collector standing at the back of the temple begging for mercy who goes home acquitted and not the Pharisee who openly gives God thanks. The temple no longer sets the rules.

"No prophet is welcome on his home turf" because there the rules are known. So one is homeless. Unlike the Foxes Who Have Dens, the son of Adam has no place to lay his head. Jesus' probable conflict with his family and village belongs to this node.

What is one to do in a situation where leaven represents the Empire of God, when what goes into a person does not defile, where toll collectors go home acquitted, the poor are congratulated and home has disappeared? "You must be as sly as a snake and as simple as a dove."

NODE TWO The Empty Jar

In contrast with the Leaven, the parable of the Empty Jar barely made the list of authentic sayings of Jesus compiled by

Node Two

Anxieties: birds
Luke 12:24, Matt 6:26
Anxieties: don't fret
Thom 36:1, Luke 12:22-23, Matt 6:25
Anxieties: clothing
Matt 6:28
Anxieties: lilies
Luke 12:27-28, Matt 6:28-30, Thom 36:2
Anxieties: one hour
Luke 12:25, Matt 6:27
Congratulations: poor
Luke 6:20, Thom 54, Matt 5:3
Corrupt judge
Luke 18:2-5
Empty jar
Thom 97:1-4
Finger of God
Luke 11:19-20, Matt 12:27-28
God's imperial rule
Thom 113:2-4, Luke 17:20-21
Lost sheep
Luke 15:4-6, Matt 18:12-13
Mustard seed
Thom 20:2-4, Mark 4:30-32, Luke 13:18-19, Matt 13:31-32
Rich farmer
Thom 63:1-6, Luke 12:16-20
Satan divided
Luke 11:17-18, Matt 12:25-26
Seed and harvest
Mark 4:26-29
Sower
Mark 4:3-8, Matt 13:3-8, Thom 9:1-5, Luke 8:5-8
Unforgiving slave
Matt 18:23-34

The texts that provide the database for the second node of relative historical certainty, leading to the insight that in God's Empire, God is present in absence.

the Jesus Seminar. There are several reasons for this. The parable occurs only in Thomas, and scholars have accorded it little concern. While these two reasons alone make me hesitant to build a significant aspect of my profile on this parable, I still think it unambiguously makes an important point.

INSIGHT God is present in absence

At the most elementary discourse level the parable is about loss. The woman starts out with a jar full of grain but arrives home empty-handed. "The handle of the jar broke ... She didn't know it ... she put the jar down and discovered that it was empty." The Empire is identified with loss, with accident, with emptiness.

It is also possible that the story of Elijah's miracle for the widow of Zarephath (1 Kings 17:8–16) lies in the background, furnishing a contrast story to the parable. During a famine a widow feeds Elijah. When he first approaches her she says, "I have nothing baked, only a handful of meal in a jar, and a little oil in a cruse." Elijah commands her to bake but bring him the first cake. "For thus says the Lord the God of Israel, 'The jar of meal shall not be spent ... until the day that the Lord sends rain upon the earth.'" She does as Elijah commands, and the prophet, she, and her child have food throughout the famine. The parable of the Empty Jar presents a contrast to the story of the widow with a full jar. There is no prophet to come to her aid, no end-time miracle to set things aright.

Even if I am not correct about the Elijah counter-reference, the basic narrative is clear. There is no divine intervention; she goes home empty-handed. This leads me to my second foundational insight: the Empire of God is identified not with divine intervention but divine emptiness. Recasting the insight will help to bring it into focus. God is not found in the apocalyptic miracle. One must look elsewhere.

This parable fills out aspects of the profile intimated in the Leaven. Like the leaven it identifies the Empire of God with the marginalized, the female, the unclean. In the end all is leavened, the jar is empty.

CONVERGENCE Spread out but not seen

The saying that most obviously belongs to this node is the Coming of God's Imperial Rule. This saying explicitly rejects the ability of people to point to or observe the Empire of God. "On the contrary, God's imperial rule is right there in your presence." Both the Thomas and Lukan versions of the saying agree on these two basic points: you cannot point to it, yet it is here. This presence of the Empire of God, unobserved but in your presence, spread out upon the earth but not seen, indicates the paradox that the Empire of God is present in absence. There is divine action in the Empire of God, but it cannot be observed.

The first Congratulation helps us understand this node of affirmations. The saying "Congratulations, you poor! God's domain belongs to you." says they are in the Empire of God and are still poor. It does not say, "Blessed are the poor, for they shall be middle class." The activity of God will not be manifest in a change from poor to rich. It is manifest in the paradox that to the poor belongs the Empire of God. To say that God is present in absence is the same as saying that to the poor belongs the Empire of God.

Likewise, in the Mustard Seed the plant does not become the great cedar of Lebanon, the more appropriate metaphor for an empire. The mustard plant is more like a weed. In the parable of the Seed and Harvest, the harvest belongs to a farmer who does not quite know what is going on. He does not observe the activity of God because he is asleep. But the last line of the parable quotes a passage in Joel about the end-time, apocalyptic war. "Prepare war, . . . Beat your plowshares into swords and your pruning forks into spears; . . . Put in the sickle, for the harvest is ripe" (Joel 3:9–13). When the farmer puts in his sickle the occasion is not the ultimate end-time war between nations, but the actions of a farmer who is simply bringing the harvest in. Even though the parable of the Sower moves towards an expectation of a dramatic harvest as a climax to its stages of failure, the harvest is quite ordinary. It is not a harvest in which one grape makes five and twenty measures of wine, as in the Rabbinic speculations on the great harvest.

If images of apocalyptic expectation are rejected, the observer will need to be very sharp-eyed. Instead of guarding the ninety-nine, the shepherd may abandon the whole flock for the one that wandered away (Lost Sheep). Not a very good bargain. And the judge who does not fear God may be the one to vindicate the widow (Corrupt Judge). It may even be dangerous to ask for God's intervention. In the parable of the Unforgiving Slave, after the king forgives the slave an astronomical debt, his fellow slaves observe his own lack of forgiveness of another slave, who by comparison owes a very small amount. They go and tell the king, who takes back his forgiveness of the debt and turns the man over to the torturers. This king is a real Hellenistic tyrant. By turning in the first slave, his fellow slaves have done the same thing to him that he had done to the slave who owed him a debt. And these fellow slaves turned him over in the name of a greater justice. The king-tyrant has made the situation even worse. Now they are dealing with a real autocrat. They have no criteria for his behavior. He may forgive everything or take it all back.

What is one to do in such a situation? One has to be very observant and see what is actually there. "Grapes are not harvested from thorn trees, nor are figs gathered from thistles" (from the complex On Anxieties: Don't Fret). The whole complexes of various sayings that deal with anxiety fit in here (Don't Fret, Lilies, Birds, Clothing, One Hour). One should not worry about clothes or eating or anything else.

The parable of the Rich Farmer tells the other side of this story. After a bounteous harvest, he has torn down his barns and builds new ones. Yet that night he must die. His anxiety did him no good. Both the parables of the Empty Jar and the Rich Farmer move from bounty (full jar, great harvest) to loss (empty jar, death).

Several recent studies of Jesus have put the healings and exorcisms of Jesus at the heart of their reconstruction. Even though it is difficult to trace individual stories of healing and exorcisms back to the earliest levels of the Jesus tradition, there can be no doubt that Jesus was a healer and exorcist. How does that activity of Jesus fit into this node? Does it not seem to contradict it?

The most explicit saying in which Jesus refers to his exorcisms equates what he does with the finger of God. "If by God's finger I drive out demons, then for you God's imperial rule has arrived." The phrase "finger of God" is used in the story of Moses' contest with the magicians of Pharaoh's court. When Aaron strikes the dust, a great swarm of gnats appears.

Unable to duplicate the feat, the magicians tell Pharaoh, "This is the finger of God" (Exod 8:19). Jesus' exorcisms bear the same relationship to Moses' wonder-working as the Mustard Plant does to the great cedar of Lebanon. Both burlesque expectations.

In a similar vein, the saying about Satan's house being divided against itself (Satan Divided) indicates that there were those who saw Jesus' activity as that of Satan himself. Thus the purported activity of God in Jesus' own exorcisms is not obviously God's activity. Perhaps this is the context in which one should view Jesus' claim to have seen Satan Falling from Heaven like lightning. Like lightning Satan was there and disappeared. Jesus' healings and exorcisms are viewed by him as divine activities, but they are not the overwhelming activities of Moses nor does his wonder-working fill up the empty jar. It still demands insight on the part of the audience. He begins by saying "If by the finger of God" indicating that the viewer must judge what kind of activity this is. And some will judge it to be the activity of Satan.

NODE THREE From Jerusalem to Jericho

The Samaritan received a very high vote of confidence from the Jesus Seminar even though only a single version survives in the gospel of Luke. This parable, among the most frequent topics in Christian art, is also one of the most popular in the tradition.

INSIGHT Cooperation, not competition

To understand this narrative we must adopt the point of view of a Jewish audience, and thus firmly set aside the gentile perspective in which the Samaritan is a good fellow, as Luke and the tradition have insisted. From the perspective of a first-century Palestinian audience, the Samaritan is the expected opponent or villain—the moral equivalent of Leaven. And his role as the hero (instead of the priest or Levite or even the anticipated "Israelite") is the same as finding the jar empty. Furthermore, this parable envisions interpersonal relations on a

Node Three

Bury the dead
Matt 8:22, Luke 9:59-60

Children in God's domain
Mark 10:14, Matt 19:14, Luke 18:16

Coat and shirt
Matt 5:40, Luke 6:29

Congratulations: hungry
Luke 6:21, Matt 5:6, Thom 69:2

Congratulations: sad
Luke 6:21, Matt 5:4

Dinner party
Thom 64:1-11, Luke 14:16-23

Emperor and God
Thom 100:2, Mark 12:17, Luke 20:25, Matt 22:21

Give to beggars
Matt 5:42, Luke 6:30

God as father
Luke 11:2, Matt 6:9

Hating one's family
Luke 14:26

Leased vineyard
Thom 65:1-7

Left and right hands
Matt 6:3, Thom 62:2

Lend without return
Thom 95:1-2, Matt 5:42

Love your enemies
Luke 6:27, Matt 5:44, Luke 6:32,35

Other cheek
Matt 5:39, Luke 6:29

Prodigal sons
Luke 15:11-32

Rich farmer
Thom 63:1-6, Luke 12:16-20

Samaritan
Luke 10:30-35

Saving one's life
Luke 17:33

Second mile
Matt 5:41

True relatives
Matt 12:48-50, Thom 99:2, Luke 8:21

Two masters
Luke 16:13, Matt 6:24, Thom 47:2, Luke 16:13,
    Matt 6:24

Vineyard laborers
Matt 20:1-15

The texts that provide the database for the third node of relative historical certainty, leading to the insight that in the world envisioned by Jesus, cooperation, not competition, is the basis for human social structure.

basis other than that of agonistic contest, or competition. Since
in the Mediterranean culture of Jesus' time all goods were
viewed as limited and fixed, relations of all types were com-
petitive or agonistic: one was always engaged in a contest for
a share of limited goods. To view this parable as anything but
a fantasy, a hearer must accept the Samaritan as helper-hero
instead of expected opponent-villain, and oneself as victim
in the ditch. An audience is not even offered the opportunity
of a contest in the narrative. The man in the ditch is passive
and the Samaritan simply has compassion, effectively ending
the story in mid-narrative. The Samaritan cannot even be the
man's patron because they belong to different societies. This
leads to my third fundamental insight: the parable re-imagines
human relationships—cooperation, not competition, is the
basis for human social structure in the Empire of God.

CONVERGENCE The great leveling

Jesus' meals are probably the immediate context in which
this node found its most concrete expression. Eating together,
sharing food in a society constantly threatened by hunger and
famine, concretely demonstrated what cooperation meant.
This is the context in which I would seek to understand the
second and third Congratulations dealing with hunger and
weeping. The archetype is Congratulations to the poor. In that
beatitude there is no future in which the poor become rich.
That beatitude should guide our understanding of the other
two. "You will have a feast" and "You will laugh" do not refer
to the apocalyptic future, but to the practice of cooperation
within the meal events. There all will share what they have. So
profound is this cooperation, so deep does it reach into the
established structures of first-century reality, that the Samaritan
can be envisioned as the hero-helper, and one can be com-
manded to "Love your enemies."

The other side of this occurs in the Rich Farmer. He
exposes himself as an epicurean. "Then I'll say to myself, 'You
have plenty put away for years to come. Take it easy, eat, drink,
enjoy yourself.'" He co-opts a fantastic harvest for himself. But
that night he dies, and so his harvest, like Joseph's in Egypt,
will be available for the village. God does intervene in this

parable, but to the villagers who helped their rich neighbor build new barns, his death will be a natural one, and they will mourn for this generous man who has provided for them. They will not have seen the hand of God in his death, though without it they would have starved. The rich man intended to keep the whole harvest for himself.

The saying about Children in God's Domain indicates those who people the Empire of God. Children are an appropriate image because they cannot play the adult roles that are being rejected as inappropriate for life in the Empire. The recasting of the family is fundamental to the redefinition of community. True Relatives are no longer one's natural family, but "Those here who do what my Father wants are my brothers and my mother." The other side of this redefinition of family is the very Hating of One's Family. There is even the abandonment of a fundamental familial duty to bury the dead: "Leave it to the dead to bury their own dead."

This re-envisioned family contains a re-imagining of God as Father. The Seminar voted overwhelmingly that Jesus used "Abba" to refer to God as father. Regardless of how Abba is to be understood, clearly the tenor of "father" as a metaphor for God is very different from that implicit in "Our Father in heaven." The latter is part of the patriarchal, patron-client world; the former is an effort to redefine family.

The parable of the Prodigal Sons exhibits in great detail a narrative of this re-imagined family. The father in the parable plays at times a foolish and shameless role and at other times a "female" role. From the very beginning of the narrative he exhibits little in the way of male honor. The admonition of Sirach about the distribution of inheritance is clear:

> While you are still alive and have breath in you, do not let any one take your place. It is better that your children should ask from you than that you should look to the hands of your sons. . . . At the time when you end the days of your life, in the hour of death, distribute your inheritance. (Sir 33:21–23)

The father in the Prodigal Son surrenders his property, a foolish act that puts both himself and his family at risk. He runs and kisses his disgraced son instead of maintaining his male dignity. He addresses the elder son as "baby."

This shameful aspect of the father has been thoroughly hidden in the history of scholarship. Even more noteworthy is that the father does not choose between his sons. He accepts both regardless of what they do. The acceptance of one is not purchased by means of the rejection of the other, a motif that is the constant pattern of such stories of elder and younger sons in the Hebrew Bible.

Finally, there is a third act implied but unspoken in the narrative. The story ends with a younger son who thinks he has struck a clever bargain with the father, now feasting on the fatted calf and enjoying all the signs of acceptance: shoes on his feet, a signet ring on his finger, and the father's best robe as his garment. Meanwhile outside waits an angry elder son who still has all the property. What happens when the father dies? If the sons continue on their present trajectories, with the younger pushing the boundaries and the elder feeling himself the abused family slave, they will kill each other. Or they can emulate the father. He is all forgiveness. There is nothing the sons can do that he will not forgive, regardless of the cost to him. He is willing to surrender all his male honor to keep both his sons in the family. Or as another saying has it, "Whoever tries to hang on to life will forfeit it, but whoever forfeits it will preserve it" (Saving One's Life).

Exactly what is at stake in the parable of the Leased Vineyard is not very clear, but it surely represents an agonistic contest run amuck. The owner who relies on the respect due him as a patron and social superior misjudges the intent of those who have leased his vineyard. These also calculate that they can get away with their acts of violence. The parable exhibits how bankrupt is a world based on competition. It is a world of unending violence.

In the Vineyard Laborers the first hired complain that by paying the last hired the same amount they have received, the master has made them equal. The laborers' complaint is that the master has destroyed the order of the world. The entire Roman Empire was organized as patron-client system. The ultimate patron was the emperor, and the system worked its way downward, with his clients in turn becoming patrons for yet other clients. So that their fleas have fleas too. Such a system ensures a hierarchically arranged social order in which no one is equal to another, and every social engagement is a contest to determine one's place in the hierarchy.

The Empire of God as family brings everyone to the same level. We see this from the rich man's point of view in the Dinner Party. In order to throw his party, he must invite the homeless and forfeit the company of those rich like himself. So radical is the disconnect between these two ways of organizing social relations that one cannot have Two Masters, something demanded by the patron-client organization of society. Calculating which master to please is a hazard of everyday life. The organization of the emperor's world is diametrically opposed to that of God's. "Give to the emperor what belongs to the emperor, give God what belongs to God."

This re-imaging of social relations finds one of its clearest expressions in those sayings burlesquing case law: Other Cheek, Coat and Shirt, Second Mile, Give to Beggars, Lend without Return. The purpose of case law is to work out in advance and in detail all the situations or cases implied by a law. These sayings of Jesus burlesque case law through a similar form and strategy. If someone demands your shirt, give him also your coat. In such a case one would be naked. If you turn the other cheek, you would soon be black and blue, beaten about the face. And finally, if you gave every time someone begged, you soon would be broke. These examples all subvert the very effort of case law to specify what is moral. "When you give charity, don't let your left hand know what your right hand is doing."

Outcomes

The world implied in these three nodes re-imagines a community's social experience. The Empire of God as Leaven does not warrant a license to do whatever one wants. Rather the unclean are accepted and welcomed by God as they are, without the necessity of becoming clean. Likewise when the Empire of God is an empty jar, then the community must accept responsibility for its life and not fall back on the nar-

cotic of a divine intervention to set things aright. When the
Samaritan is the hero-helper, then social cooperation is defined
outside the bounds of the traditional patron-client relationship.
These three aspects go a long way towards redefining basic
human relationships within a Mediterranean peasant culture.

The Empire as Symbol

The Empire of God is at the core of Jesus' re-imagining. It is
the presiding symbol, whether or not it is always or ever the
referent of the parables. Also the understanding of the Empire
of God must be derived from Jesus' language-activity, rather
than from a historical survey of Jewish literature. Such a survey
produces little fruit because of the very infrequent appearance of the phrase. As a symbol, Empire of God stands for the
experience that results from the language-activity of Jesus. The
Coming of God's Imperial Rule clearly indicates that it is a
non-empirical reality. "You won't be able to observe the coming of God's imperial rule. People are not going to be able to
say, 'Look, here it is!' or 'Over there.'"

Jesus surely uses Empire in an ironical sense since the
Empire of God fails to measure up when compared to the
empires of David or Caesar. This irony and non-compari-
son is clearly represented in the emperor and God: "Give the
emperor what belongs to the emperor, give God what belongs
to God." So negatively, the Empire of God is not like the
empires of David or Caesar. As a symbol, the Empire of God is
like the American flag. It stands for a whole series of complex
values that cannot be expressed clearly—that is why one needs
to employ a symbol to represent it. But to go even further, I
think the Empire of God functions to create a sphere in the
imagination in which those who are a part of this community
of envisioning can experience healing, the welcome of the
unclean, the presence of God in God's non-empirical activity.

The Death of Jesus

The reason(s) for the death of Jesus probably remain beyond
our grasp. Empires can and do act in authoritarian ways that

escape the cool rationality of law or reason. Pilate did not really need a worked out case to kill Jesus. Yet one can see in Jesus' language-activity the seeds of a conflict that could easily escalate to a confrontation and to death. The parable of the Leaven and what it implies are sufficient blasphemy to put Jesus into conflict with the religious authorities. For them the symbol of God's activity is unleaven, the clean. The leaven must be cleaned out to make a place pure and holy, set apart. And even though Jesus explicitly separates God's Empire and Caesar's, the success of Jesus' social experiment in peasant community under the symbol of the Empire of God would pose a threat to Rome's rule, a rule built on the premise that the local population is divided and distrustful of each other. A peasantry that accepts each other, that no longer sees itself in conflict with each other, always defending their given and limited positions, even reaching out to Samaritan enemies, poses a real threat to Rome's rule by thwarting its attempts to divide and conquer.

JESUS AS REBEL
A Social Science Model

One of the most perplexing problems in the quest for the historical Jesus is why Jesus opted for such a radical program. Frequently interpreters avoid this problem and fall back on the inevitability of history. What happened had to happen. But, of course, that is not true; it is the fallacy of the inevitable. Like most peasants in his situation, Jesus could have done nothing. At other times I suspect that an assumed Christology warrants the model. That is to say, we fall back unthinkingly on faith commitments as though those explain why Jesus opted for such a radical program.

What complicates any attempted solution to the problem is the very lack of data. We know almost nothing about Jesus' interior life, his psychological or social development. Nor do we even possess a chronological narrative in which to arrange a "life of Jesus."

Social science methods have provided a way forward. Crossan, for example, presents in The Historical Jesus a model of brokerage in the Roman Empire that produced a system on the verge of breakdown. But what Crossan has explained is why the Roman Empire was such an unstable society and why the Jews revolted in 68 CE. What a social model cannot explain is why an individual decides to revolt. Social sciences deal with social groups, not individuals.

JESUS AS REBEL
A Family Dynamics Model

What we need is a model to help explain why an individual revolts. Frank Sulloway in *Born to Rebel* has argued that family dynamics, not social class, are the most important variables in explaining an individual's proclivity to revolt. For Sulloway, most important aspect in the model is birth order. Latterborn children are more likely to be rebels because of the internal evolutionary dynamics of family life. Children have to find a niche in the family structure in order to prove their value to their parents. Parents invest most heavily in the firstborn, and to be more precise, the firstborn male in traditional societies. Thus the firstborn does not have to search for a niche and automatically receives a high investment from the parents. Firstborns more naturally identify strongly with power and authority. Latterborns must find their own niche in the family, so in order to succeed they must be open to experience.

Openness to experience is a term psychologists employ to indicate a crucial aspect of the creative process. "People who exhibit openness are described as imaginative, flexible, creative, independent, and liberal" (20). Birth order, gender, and temperament interact to produce personality characteristics. These are, in Sulloway's argument, more determinant of the creative individual than social class. If social class were the dominant factor we would expect siblings to be very similar. Yet "siblings raised together are almost as different in their personalities as people from different families" (xiii). Thus family structure produces the difference.

In the development of his thesis Sulloway argues from the centrality of birth order, but other factors in a family's dynam-

ics make the model more predictive. By itself, the birth order
will not correctly predict openness to experience any more
accurately than will flipping a coin. But when combined with
other factors, for example, conflict with a parent, then the
predictive power rises substantially.

Sulloway's model can be used negatively to call into question certain assumptions. Meier, for example, envisions Jesus
as the firstborn, raised in an intact family, with Joseph teaching his son Jesus his trade and schooling him in Hebrew and
the traditions of Judaism. If this were in fact the case, then the
chance that Jesus would lead a radical revolution would be less
than two percent according to Sulloway's evidence. So that
traditional assumption about Jesus' birth order and family situation can be set aside.

The tradition of Jesus as the firstborn very probably results
from faith speculating about the significance of Jesus and not
family remembrance. James may well be the elder brother of
Jesus and in fact what little we know of him would support
this theory. His assumption of power and the maintenance of
family authority in Jerusalem result from the adaptive strategies
of a firstborn.

We can also use Sulloway's model to sort and evaluate some
of the items about Jesus' family relations contained in the gospels. Sulloway notes that the death of a parent or a missing
parent has a strong effect on siblings. The firstborn becomes
more conservative, the latterborn more open to experience,
more likely to rebel. The existence of Joseph has been deemed
problematic since he appears only in the later stages of the tradition, making no appearance in Mark or the Sayings Gospel
Q, and having no function in the sayings of Jesus. This absence
of Joseph during the life of Jesus led later Christians to speculate that he was an old man when he married Mary and had
died by the time Jesus was active. Since Joseph is surely a later
fiction of the gospel writers, we have no good evidence for
Jesus' father. Jane Schaberg has argued that the birth of Jesus
was illegitimate. Whatever the facts about Jesus' father, his
absence from the family would have had a strong impact on
the siblings, inclining Jesus to rebel.

Finally there is evidence in the tradition of conflict between Jesus and his own family. Clearly, the family of Jesus is not part of his original group of followers. These three factors, latterborn birth rank, absence of a father, and conflict with the family would in Sulloway's model put Jesus in the group most likely to exhibit a radical response.

Sulloway's model offers a way to begin to sort out some of these issues and clarify what we can and cannot explain. The interface between historical, social scientific models and the family dynamics model is very important. The historical-social model provides evidence about the specific cognitive and ideological structures that make up a culture. Family dynamics helps us understand how an individual responds to that structure—why some support the structure, while others revolt.

Jesus as Poet

Jesus' revolt takes a very special form. He revolts in parable. I see no evidence that Jesus was leading a political revolution or that he had a social program in mind. He clearly affected the lives of people, but he was not a social organizer or activist. Although the view is now out of fashion, Jesus seems to me closer to the poet. The activist will always be dissatisfied with the poetic vision, but change comes about because a creative individual has a vision.

That vision as I have tried to sketch it out in this profile has much in common with the poetic vision. Seamus Heaney has recently addressed this issue in his *The Redress of Poetry*. I take the liberty of quoting a passage that is to the point.

> And in the activity of poetry too, there is a tendency to place a counter-reality in the scales—a reality which may be only imagined but which nevertheless has weight because it is imagined within the gravitational pull of the actual and can therefore hold its own and balance out against the historical situation. This redressing effect of poetry comes from its being a glimpsed alternative, a revelation of potential that is denied or constantly threatened by circumstances. And sometimes, of course, it hap-

pens that such a revelation, once enshrined in the poem, remains as a standard for the poet, so that he or she must then submit to the strain of bearing witness in his or her own life to the place of consciousness established in the poem. (pp. 3–4)

Heaney has captured in his understanding of the redress of poetry an insight into how Jesus' language offered to his audience an alternative to the world in which they were trapped. It was a world burdened by purity laws segregating the unclean from the clean and thus creating further degrees of purity or shame; a world where those on the bottom are imprisoned in unchangeable structures and await a divine solution; a world in which enemies threaten at every point.

Jesus in his language offers a counter world, a vision, an openness to experience. It is a "glimpsed alternative, a revelation of potential that is denied or constantly threatened by circumstances." It may be only an imagined or re-imagined alternative, but it derives its weight from its opposition to and careful observation of the historical world. Apart from the gravitational pull of that historical world, Jesus' glimpsed alternative is without meaning or open to whatever one wants it to mean.

Several scholars have strongly objected to a view of Jesus that puts his language and parables at the center of the search for the historical Jesus. Sanders has objected "that it is difficult make his [Jesus'] teaching offensive enough to lead to execution" (4). Meier is even more acid in his remarks.

A tweedy poetaster who spent his time spinning out parables and Japanese koans, a literary aesthete who toyed with 1st century deconstructionism, or a bland Jesus who simply told people to look at the lilies of the field—such a Jesus would threaten no one, just as the university professors who create him threaten no one. (vol. 1, 177)

Perhaps Meier's remark reflects his own impotency in a capitalist society rather than an objective assessment of words in the ancient world.

Socrates, next to Jesus one of the most famous martyrs of the ancient world, died because of his provocative language, and the fate of Salman Rushdie in our own day demonstrates the power of words in a traditional society. Poets still have power. Vaclav Havel was imprisoned for his poems and plays, led the velvet revolution, and became the first president of Czechoslovakia and then of the Czech Republic. What Havel has to say about hope explains how the Empire of God functions as a revolutionary symbol for Jesus' followers. Hope, he says, is

> a state of mind, not a state of the world . . . and it's not essentially dependent on some particular observation of the world or estimate of the situation . . . it transcends the world that is immediately experienced, and is anchored somewhere beyond its horizons. . . . It is not the conviction that something will turn out well, but the certainty that something makes sense, regardless of how it turns out. (p. 181)

Jesus revolts in parable and the parables create a counter-world, a hoped-for world that redresses the world as it is and surely makes sense, regardless of how it turns out—even if it results in his crucifixion.

Works Consulted

Bloom, Harold. *Hamlet: Poem Unlimited*. New York: Riverhead Books, Penguin Putnam, Inc., 2003.

_____. *How to Read and Why*. New York: Touchstone Books, 2001.

_____. *Shakespeare: The Invention of the Human*. New York: Riverhead Books, 1998.

Borg, Marcus J. *Jesus in Contemporary Scholarship*. Valley Forge, PA: Trinity Press International, 1994.

_____. *Meeting Jesus Again for the First Time: The Historical Jesus and the Heart of Contemporary Faith*. San Francisco: HarperSanFrancisco, 1994.

_____. *A New Vision: Spirit, Culture, and the Life of Discipleship*. San Francisco: Harper and Row, 1987.

Breech, James. *The Silence of Jesus*. Philadelphia: Fortress, 1983.

Carse, James P. *Finite and Infinite Games: A Vision of Life as Play and Possibility*. New York: Ballantine, 1987.

Collins, Billy. *Questions about Angels*. Pittsburgh: University of Pittsburgh Press, 1991.

Crossan, John Dominic. *The Dark Interval: Towards a Theology of Story*. Sonoma, CA: Polebridge, 1988.

_____. *Finding Is the First Act*. Semeia Supplements. Philadelphia: Fortress Press, 1979.

_____. *The Historical Jesus: The Life of a Mediterranean Jewish Peasant*. San Francisco: HarperSanFrancisco, 1991.

_____. *In Parables*. New York: Harper & Row, 1973.

_____. *Jesus: A Revolutionary Biography*. San Francisco: HarperSanFrancisco, 1994.

Dodd, C. H. *The Parables of the Kingdom*. New York: Charles Scribner's Sons, 1961.

Donahue, John R. *The Gospel in Parable*. Philadelphia: Fortress Press, 1988.

Fisher, Neal F. *The Parables of Jesus: Glimpses of God's Reign.* New York: Crossroad, 1990.

Francis, Robert. *The Orb Weaver.* Middletown, CT: Wesleyan University Press, 1960.

Frye, Northrop. *Anatomy of Criticism.* Princeton, NJ: Princeton University Press, 1957.

_____. *The Double Vision: Language and Meaning in Religion.* Toronto: University of Toronto Press, 1991.

Funk, Robert W. *A Credible Jesus: Fragments of a Vision.* Santa Rosa, CA: Polebridge Press, 2002.

_____, Roy W. Hoover, and the Jesus Seminar. *The Five Gospels: The Search for the Authentic Words of Jesus.* New York: Scribners, 1993.

_____ *Funk on Parables.* Edited by Bernard Brandon Scott. Santa Rosa: Polebridge, 2006.

_____. *Honest to Jesus: Jesus for the New Millennium.* San Francisco: HarperSanFrancisco, 1996.

_____. *Jesus as Precursor.* Philadelphia: Fortress Press, 1975; Rev. ed., Edward F. Beutner, ed. Sonoma, CA: Polebridge, 1994.

_____. *Language, Hermeneutic, and Word of God.* New York: Harper & Row, 1966.

_____. *Parables and Presence.* Philadelphia: Fortress Press, 1982.

_____, Bernard Brandon Scott, and James R. Butts, eds. *The Parables of Jesus: A Report of the Jesus Seminar.* Sonoma: Polebridge, 1988.

Goldin, Judah, trans. *The Fathers According to Rabbi Nathan.* Yale Judaica Series. New Haven: Yale University Press, 1955.

Havel, Vaclay. *Disturbing the Peace.* London: Faber and Faber, 1990.

Heaney, Seamus. *The Redress of Poetry.* London: Faber and Faber, 1995.

Hedrick, Charles W. *Parables as Poetic Fictions: The Creative Voice of Jesus.* Peabody, MA: Hendrickson, 1994.

Herzog II, William R. *Parables as Subversive Speech: Jesus as Pedagogue of the Oppressed.* Louisville: John Knox, 1994.

Howard, Daniel F. *Lessons in Critical Reading and Writing: William Shakespeare's Hamlet.* San Francisco: Harcourt Brace Jovanovich, 1970.

Jeremias, Joachim. *The Parables of Jesus.* Translated by S. H. Hooke. New York: Charles Scribner's Sons, 1972.

Jülicher, Adolf. *Die Gleichnisreden Jesu.* Tubingen: J. C. B. Mohr (Paul Siebeck), 1910.

McFague, Sallie. *Speaking in Parables*. Philadelphia: Fortress, 1975.

Meier, John P. *A Marginal Jew: Rethinking the Historical Jesus*. 2 vols. The Anchor Bible Reference Library. Garden City: Doubleday, 1991, 1994.

Miller, Robert J., ed. *The Complete Gospels*. Santa Rosa, CA: Polebridge Press, 1994.

Perrin, Norman. *Jesus and the Language of the Kingdom*. Philadelphia: Fortress Press, 1976.

Roethke, Theodore. *The Collected Poems of Theodore Roethke*. New York: Anchor Books, 1975.

Sanders, E. P. *Jesus and Judaism*. Philadelphia: Fortress Press, 1985.

Schaberg, Jane. *The Illegitimacy of Jesus*. San Francisco: Harper and Row, 1987.

Schneiders, Sandra M. *The Revelatory Text: Interpreting the New Testament as Sacred Scriptures*. San Francisco: HarperSanFrancisco, 1991.

Scott, Bernard Brandon. "From Reimarus to Crossan: Stages in a Quest." *Currents in Research: Biblical Studies* 2 (1994): 253–80.

_____. *Hear Then the Parable*. Minneapolis: Augsburg Fortress, 1989.

_____. *Jesus: Symbol-Maker for the Kingdom*. Philadelphia: Fortress, 1981.

_____. *Re-Imagine the World: An Introduction to the Parables of Jesus*. Santa Rosa, CA: Polebridge Press, 2001.

Sulloway, Frank J. *Born to Rebel: Birth Order, Family Dynamics, and Creative Lives*. New York: Pantheon Books, 1996.

Tatum, W. Barnes. *Jesus at the Movies: A Guide to the First Hundred Years*. Santa Rosa, CA: Polebridge Press, 1997.

_____. *John the Baptist and Jesus: A Jesus Seminar Report*. Sonoma, CA: Polebridge Press, 1994.

Wilder, Amos. *The Bible and the Literary Critic*. Minneapolis: Fortress, 1991.

_____. *The Language of the Gospel*. New York: Harper & Row, 1964.

Questions
for Discussion

Introduction
Edward F. Beutner, *The Haunt of the Parable*

1. Traditionally we have thought of Jesus as a teacher and the parables as his teaching. What is Beutner suggesting when he claims that parables' purpose is to haunt?
2. What does it mean to "drop a mouse" into a parable, rather than try to force meaning out if?

Chapter 1
Lane C. McGaughy, *Jesus' Parables and the Fiction of the Kingdom*

1. How does the two-storied universe of Greek myth support allegory?
2. Since, in a metaphor, there is no direct connection between the subject and object, how is the connection made? For example, "My love is a red rose," is not literally true. So how is it true?
3. In allegory the characters of a story have a meaning or referent from outside the story. For example, the referent for master is God. If the parable is a metaphor, how does this change the meaning or how one finds the meaning?
4. The parable as metaphor leads to an unexpected conclusion. How does this lead to an experience of a new reality in language?
5. The unexpected conclusion of the parable makes it open-ended. It has no single interpretation but a multitude of interpretations. Of the various possible interpretations how do you know which ones are correct?

Chapter 2
Edward F. Beutner, *How Jesus Took the Gist from Liturgist*

1. What does Beutner imply when he says that Jesus appears inordinately fond of hanging out? What is the implied contrast?
2. What are some examples of modern "social maps" or "social scripts"?
3. What would a "moralistic" interpretation of the parable of the Pharisee and tax collector look like?
4. What, if anything, is wrong with the prayer of the Pharisee? Remember the trap of moralizing.
5. In what way does the parable interpret the reader (hearer), rather than the reader (hearer) interpret the parable? Or is this just another parable?

Chapter 3
Bernard Brandon Scott, *On the Road Again*

1. Make a list of violent acts that occur in Jesus' parables. How does this list fit with the popular image of gentle Jesus. What does it tell us about the world Jesus lived in?
2. In what way is Mark's interpretation of the parable of the Leased Vineyard an allegory?
3. If Jesus' parable warns against the use of violence to claim or bring God's kingdom, what myths or beliefs in the Jewish and Christian traditions does this reject?

Chapter 4
Edward F. Beutner, *A Mercy Unextended*

1. How does the Robert Francis poem "Pitcher" help you understand Jesus the parable teller? Does it mislead you in any way?
2. Why does Beutner argue that God is "cast *outside* the parable"?
3. How is the behavior of the king (drug lord) different from that of God?
4. Does this essay show how Jesus was betrayed by his speech, as Beutner's opening paragraph notes?

Chapter 5
Paul Verhoeven, *The First Will Be First*

1. Verhoeven argues that originally the parable started with the payment of those hired first. How strong do you think his argument is? What are its weaknesses? If you were voting in the Jesus Seminar, what color would you give his reconstruction? Red? Pink? Gray? or Black?
2. If Verhoeven is correct in his reordering of the payment, why would Matthew have changed it?
3. What effect does Verhoeven's re-ordering of the payment have on the parable's interpretation or meaning?
4. Why does Miller insist that the owner is generous if a denarius a day is the standard wage?
5. What are the various reasons for the master to return to the marketplace to hire more workers?
6. After following the discussion between Verhoeven and Miller, do you think the master is good or bad?
7. Miller says, "the key question is whether Jesus' audience starts the story identifying with the owner or with the workers." Traditionally, readers have identified with the master. Why? Remember: allegory. Why is this a key question? What do you think?

Chapter 6
Edward F. Beutner, *Comedy with a Tragic Turn*

1. How does Beutner's suggestion that this parable is a comedy shift or change your previous view of the parable?
2. Beutner suggests that the parable is addressed to Galilean peasants who would see both the master and the manager as above them in social class. What effect has your social class had on your viewing of the actions of characters?

Chapter 7
Robert J. Miller, *The Pearl, the Treasure, the Fool, and the Cross*

1. If the merchant sells everything to buy the pearl, what is his next step? What are the implications of that step?

2. Miller points to two explanations for man's immoral behavior in the parable of the Treasure. The first looks for events in Jesus' life; the second points to Jesus' frequent use of characters who behave immorally. Which of these two do you find most convincing? Why do you think so many of the characters in the parables behave in problematic ways?

3. Given that the man has purchased, under false pretensions, a field with a treasure hidden it, what are his options?

4. In what ways is the *basileia* (kingdom) of God political? Why is proclaiming it dangerous?

5. In Miller's interpretation of the Treasure as reflecting Jesus' life, the accent falls on the joy of pursuing the kingdom. How, then, does one deal with the man's immoral behavior in buying the field?

Chapter 8
Edward F. Beutner, *Jesus after Hamlet*

1. In comparing Jesus and Hamlet, Beutner maintains that for both, "the method of metaphor delivers their listeners from the madness of myth." What does this mean? Give an example of it both from Jesus and from Hamlet?

2. Hamlet is a fictional character, a creation of Shakespeare. In what sense is Jesus also a fictional character?

Chapter 9
Robert W. Funk, *Jesus of Nazareth*

1. Funk describes Jesus as "the first standup Jewish comic." How is Jesus a comic?

2. Funk constructs a negative list of what Jesus was not. Can you construct a positive list of what Jesus was or was about?

Chapter 10
Bernard Brandon Scott, *The Reappearance of Parables*

1. Various authors in this volume have struggled with how to translate the *basileia* of God: kingdom, reign, imperial rule, ruling activity, empire. How do you evaluate these proposals? Which one do you prefer? Why?

2. To say that God is unclean is an oxymoron, a contradiction. How then can it generate a new insight into the divine?
3. If the empire of God cannot be pointed to, but is in your midst, within and without, how does one know what and where it is?
4. What does an empire not built on contest and aggression look like? In what sense is it an empire?
5. Scott argues that Jesus' language offers an alternative vision, a counter world. Is this world real or imaginary?